Irresistible

Gifts to
Cross Stitch

Irresistible Gifts to Cross Stitch is an original work, first published in 2011 in the United Kingdom by Future Publishing Limited in magazine form under the title *Irresistible Gifts to Cross Stitch*. This title is printed and distributed in North America under license. All rights reserved.

ISBN 978-1-57421-445-1

Printed in China
First printing

Irresistible Gifts to Cross Stitch

Inspired Designs and Patterns for Hand-Stitched Projects to Make and Give

Editors of **CrossStitcher**

Design Originals

an Imprint of Fox Chapel Publishing

www.d-originals.com

Contents

106

24

88

117

82

Introduction

WELCOME TO THE ULTIMATE COLLECTION OF GORGEOUS GOODIES TO STITCH AND SHARE ALL YEAR ROUND! Making gifts is the perfect excuse to stitch! In this book, you'll find gifts and cards to make that cover all of those special occasions.

Christmas is a popular time to stitch (somewhere between decorating the tree, wrapping the presents and writing to Santa!) so make time to stitch these festive cards and gifts. The bright colors and motifs in the children's chapter will definitely be a hit with all ages, from toddlers to tweens, and for new arrivals there are the sweetest keepsakes to mark the birth. Romance is forever in the air for cross stitchers – weddings, engagements and other loving moments give us the go-ahead to stitch, while there's always a date in the diary to get together with loved ones, from Mother's Day and Halloween to Easter and birthdays.

With projects suitable for all abilities, including simple instructions to turn your cross stitch into that irresistible gift, this must-have collection means you'll be ready for anything.

Happy stitching!

INSIDE...

From treats for the kids to sentimental gifts of love – it's all here!

WHAT A HOOT!
Make a colorful owl cushion for a child's bedroom – or keep him for yourself! – p24

BABY STEPS
Felt booties for a new baby – they're almost too cute to use – p16

LITTLE MONSTERS
The kids will be lining up for these collectible little buttons – p27

LOVING HEART
A little love goes a long way – p64

BABIES

CELEBRATE NEW ARRIVALS WITH BABY
BOOTIES, PERSONALIZED SAMPLERS, OR
HANDSTITCHED TREATS FOR THE NURSERY

Bear essentials

Make a new parent's day by stitching them this irresistible set of accessories for the nursery, all in neutral shades to suit baby boys and girls

Designed by: Lucie Heaton
Stitch time: 20 hours

These cuddly characters transform a simple hanger into a perfect storage solution for baby accessories. With limited stitching on a plain evenweave, this design is ideal for newbies or stitchers who aren't very experienced, but if you're more advanced or just feeling adventurous try experimenting with different colors and fabrics. Don't miss the cute matching cushions on page 11 – they're so small and light they're safe enough to be left in a baby's cot. Just make sure you fill them with something snuggly and hypoallergenic.

Or try... **this!**

Don't fancy a hanger? Make a drawstring bag instead!

A MULTI-PURPOSE bag is a lifesaver for new moms. Make one to keep all those nursery essentials in, from nappies and bottles to toys and spare socks! Back your stitching with fleece first for a sturdier finish.

Materials

Hanging

- 20 count evenweave, 26x60cm (10¼"x23¾")
- Child size wooden hanger
- Fleece backing fabric, 26x60cm (10¼"x23¾")

Photography by Neil Godwin

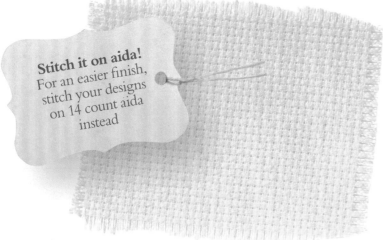

Stitch it on aida!
For an easier finish, stitch your designs on 14 count aida instead

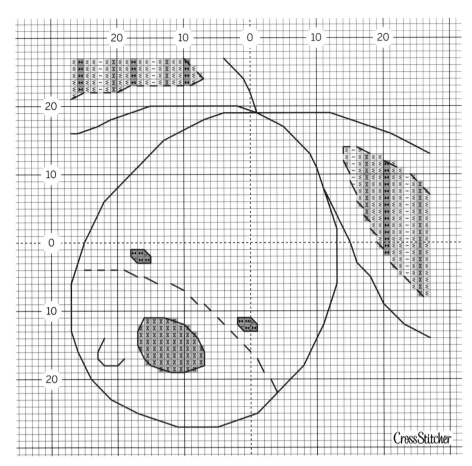

DMC	Anchor	Madeira
Cross stitch in four strands		
◄► 434	310	2009
☒ 436	363	2011
~ 712	926	2101
◄ 738	361	2013
Backstitch in two strands		
—— 898	380	2006
all details		

Make a…
hanging

Step 1
CUT your stitching to measure 26x60cm (10¼"x23¾") so that the bottom stitched edge is about 22cm (8¾") from the bottom of the fabric. Cut a piece of backing fabric to the same size. With right sides together stitch around all four sides, leaving an opening for turning.

Step 2
TURN right side out and slip stitch the opening closed. Fold the bottom edge up, just under the stitched edge, and pin in place. Machine stitch along both sides of the fold. Machine stitch a second line through the middle to create two separate pockets for storing accessories.

Step 3
TO ATTACH to your hanger, fold the top edge over the hanger and pin in place. Hand stitch in place, taking care to only sew through the backing fabric. For added security, use a couple of flat drawing pins to hold your fabric in place. If desired you can also tie cord around a dowel to create your hanger.

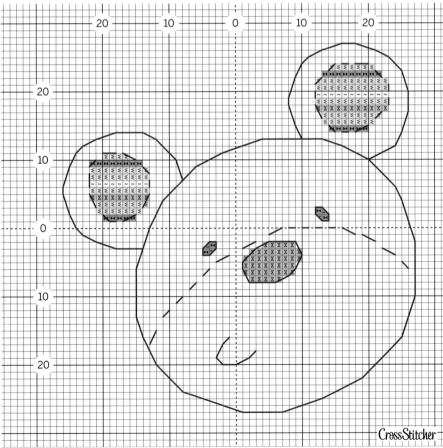

To create your mini cushions, machine stitch right up to the stitched edges to get the maximum impact from your design. When stitching this way, each cushion will end up a slightly different size

Materials

Cushions
- 20 count evenweave, two 30x30cm (12"x12") pieces
- Fleece backing fabric, 18x18cm (7¼"x7¼")
- Stuffing

Sweet hearts

Celebrate a new arrival with one of these pretty keepsakes – all you need is a fancy box to wrap it in!

Designed by: Lucie Heaton

Stitch time: 6 hours each

Photography by Neil Godwin

Make a... heart sachet

Step 1

MAKE a start by placing your design face up on a flat surface. Using colored tailor's chalk or a fading fabric pen, draw a heart-shaped sewing guideline around your design. Cut your stitched piece and backing piece 1cm (¼") wider than your guideline.

Step 2

TO stop the edges from fraying, add a zig zag stitch around the perimeter of both pieces of fabric. Fold your ribbon length in half and pin the two ends along the top edge of your stitched piece, with the loop resting on the surface of your stitching.

Step 3

TAKE your unstitched piece of evenweave and place it on top of your design, sandwiching the ribbon as you go. Pin in position before machining in place. Remember to leave an opening along one edge to fill your sachet.

Step 4

REMOVE any pins, before turning your sachet right side out. Sew a mother of pearl button to where the ribbon meets the evenweave. Fill with stuffing and lavender if desired and slipstitch the opening closed.

	DMC	Anchor	Madeira
Cross stitch in two strands			
⌡	162	1032	1104
♥	605	1094	0613
~	963	023	0503
∩	3747	120	0901
Backstitch in one strand			
——	3799	236	1713
	all outlines and details		
Stitching guide			
——	use as a guide for sewing heart seams		

FABRIC CARE

Evenweave gives much smoother finish than aida, but it frays very easily which can make it fiddlier to work with. Always add a blanket or zig zag stitch to raw edges before you begin stitching. When you've finished, cut your fabric to the appropriate shape and again finish your edges. This way your evenweave won't unravel while you're making up your sachet.

Position your name by starting with the middle letter and working out. Plan on graph paper before you begin stitching. It will prevent lots of unpicking!

Materials

- 28 count white evenweave, two 15x20cm (6"x8") pieces
- Blue or pink ribbon
- Mother-of-pearl button
- Stuffing

Stitch it on aida! If you like, stitch your designs on 14 count white aida instead.

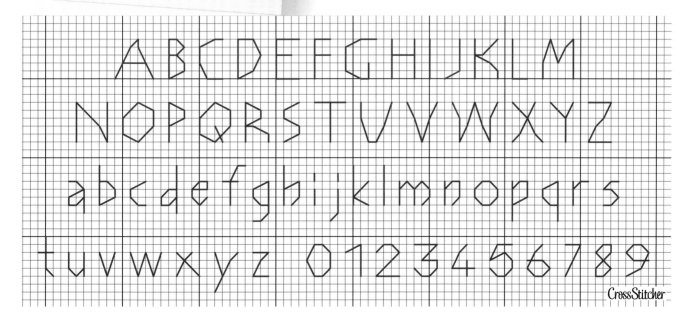

CrossStitcher

Baby Steps

These irresistible felt booties are the perfect gift for a new baby. They're almost too cute to use!

Designed by: Helen Philipps

These booties are so easy to make. You only need one piece of felt, a few waste canvas scraps – and there's hardly any sewing involved either!

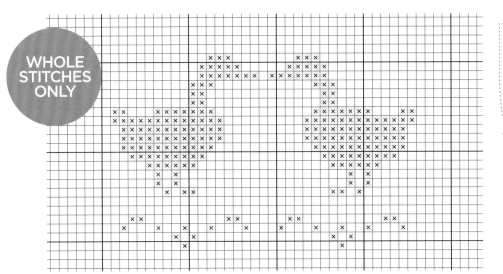

DMC	Anchor	Madeira
Cross stitch in three strands		
✗ White	002	2402

Templates

Use these shapes to create the pieces for your booties

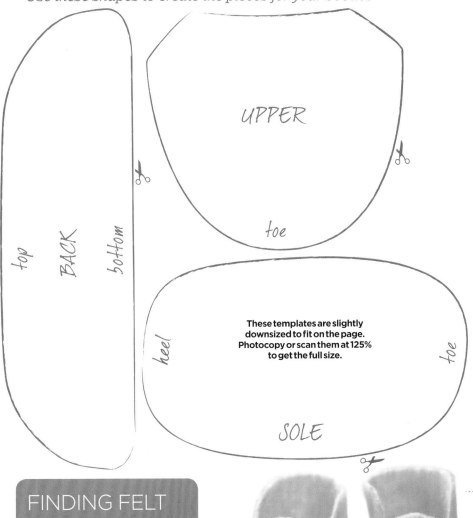

top BACK bottom

UPPER

toe

heel

These templates are slightly downsized to fit on the page. Photocopy or scan them at 125% to get the full size.

toe

SOLE

Make... baby booties

Step 1

USE the templates to cut out two felt pieces of each shape. Center your stitching in the middle of the upper pieces. Hand sew the upper piece to the sole using whip stitch. Bring your needle up from the bottom to the top, then again up from the bottom to the top, creating loops around the join.

Step 2

ATTACH the upper piece, then the back piece, to the sole. The back piece should overlap the upper piece slightly in the middle. Once you've finished, add a decorative mother-of-pearl or wooden button to both sides of the shoe, at the point where the back and upper pieces meet.

FINDING FELT

Felt is available in fabric stores by the sheet or yard. A fat quarter (18"x22") is enough to make several pairs of booties as well as lots of other felt goodies.

Materials

- Thick felt
- Waste or soluble canvas
- Four mother-of-pearl buttons

Celebrate in stripes

Welcome a new baby with one of these super-cute animal cards

Designed by: Joanne Sanderson

Stitch time: 6 hours each

Baby Girl

Baby Twins

Baby Boy

Materials

- 28 count white evenweave, 16x18cm (6½"x17¼")
- Pink, pale blue and pale green aperture cards
- White paper to back your design

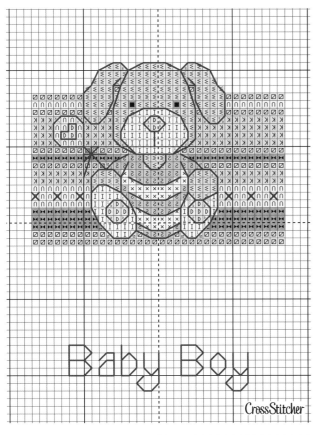

Baby Boy

CrossStitcher

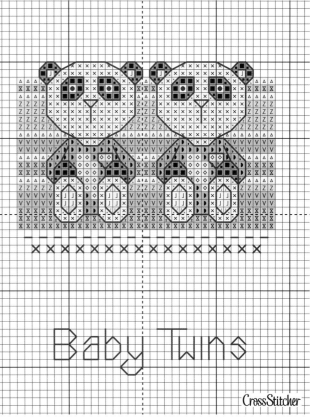

Baby Twins

CrossStitcher

Baby Girl

CrossStitcher

DMC	Anchor	Madeira
Cross stitch in two strands		
✕ White	002	2402
◗ 155	109	0803
✛ 209	108	0711
◇ 211	342	0801
■ 413	236	1713
≤ 437	362	2012
♥ 601	063	0703
I 739	366	2014
X 742	303	0114
∩ 744	301	0112
△ 745	300	0111
V 912	209	1213
♡ 957	050	0612
K 959	186	1113

DMC	Anchor	Madeira
Cross stitch in two strands		
J 963	023	0608
Z 3348	264	1409
Cross stitch in two strands		
D 3716	025	0606
⊠ 3761	928	1105
S 3840	120	0907
⋈ 3848	1074	1108
Backstitch in one strand		
—— 413	236	1713
all details		
French knots in one strand		
● 413	236	1713
panda eyes		

Make sure you stitch your design using an embroidery hoop or frame. This will keep the stripes in your design looking crisp and even

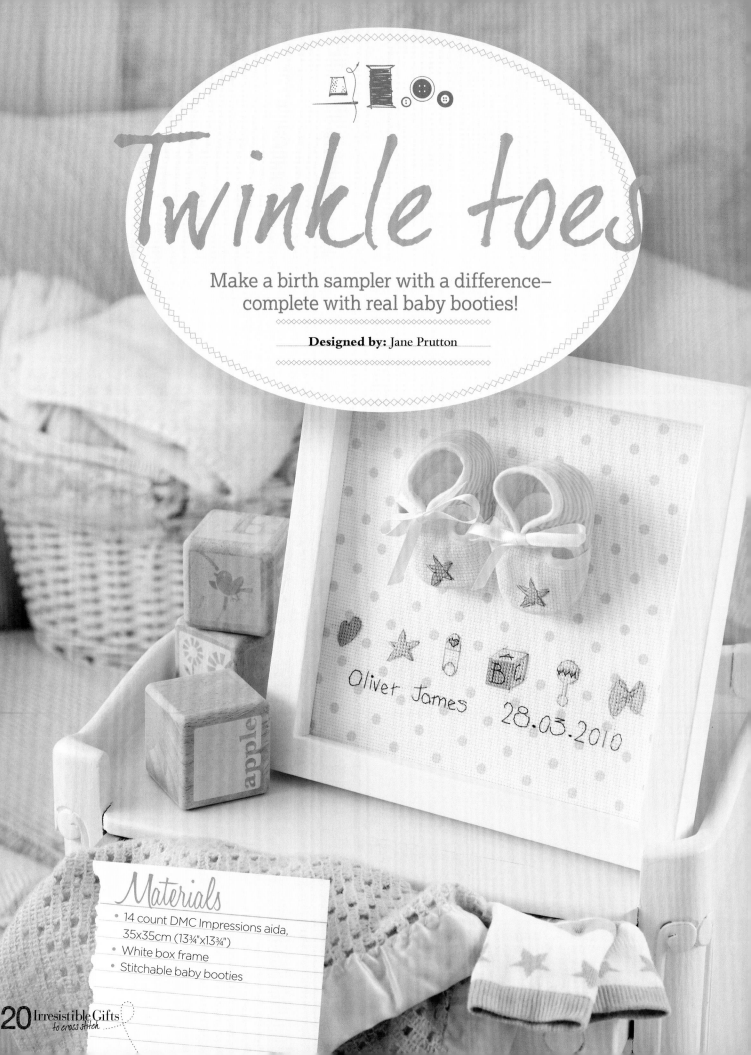

Twinkle toes

Make a birth sampler with a difference—
complete with real baby booties!

Designed by: Jane Prutton

Materials

- 14 count DMC Impressions aida, 35x35cm (13¾"x13¾")
- White box frame
- Stitchable baby booties

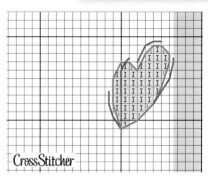

CrossStitcher

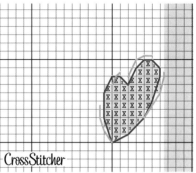

CrossStitcher

If you can't find stitchable booties, just use ordinary store-bought ones

	Anchor	DMC	Madeira
Cross stitch in two strands			
♡	025	3716	0606
▲	128	775	0908
I	253	472	1604
X	311	3855	2301
~	926	712	1908
Backstitch in one strand			
	025	3716	0606
	027	893	0413
	028	892	0412
	129	3325	0907
	134	820	0914
	145	799	0910
	For a girl:		
	028	892	0412
	For a boy:		
	134	820	0914
French knots in one strand			
●	For a girl:		
	028	892	0412
	For a boy:		
	134	820	0914

STITCHING ON BOOTIES

Stitching on ready made items like baby booties can be a bit tricky. Using a smaller needle and shorter thread lengths should help make weaving in and out of small spaces easier.

Leave four squares between the bottom of the row of motifs and the top of your lettering, and plan the lettering out on a piece of blank graph paper first

Make a...
booties sampler

Step 1

STITCH your motif and name rows so that there's 20cm (8") of excess fabric above the whole design and 10cm (4") below. Stretch your stitching around a piece of mount board so that there's about 14cm (5½") of empty space above the top of the motif row and about 4cm (1½") of space below the bottom of the name row.

Step 2

REMOVE the glass from your frame and mount your stitching. Stitch the motif of your choice on to the booties. Once you're happy with the position of the booties in the frame, stitch through the soles, the aida and the mount board to secure in place.

Step 3

TO CREATE removable booties, attach Velcro circles to the bootie soles and to your stitched piece. Don't forget to add a keepsake label to the back of your frame.

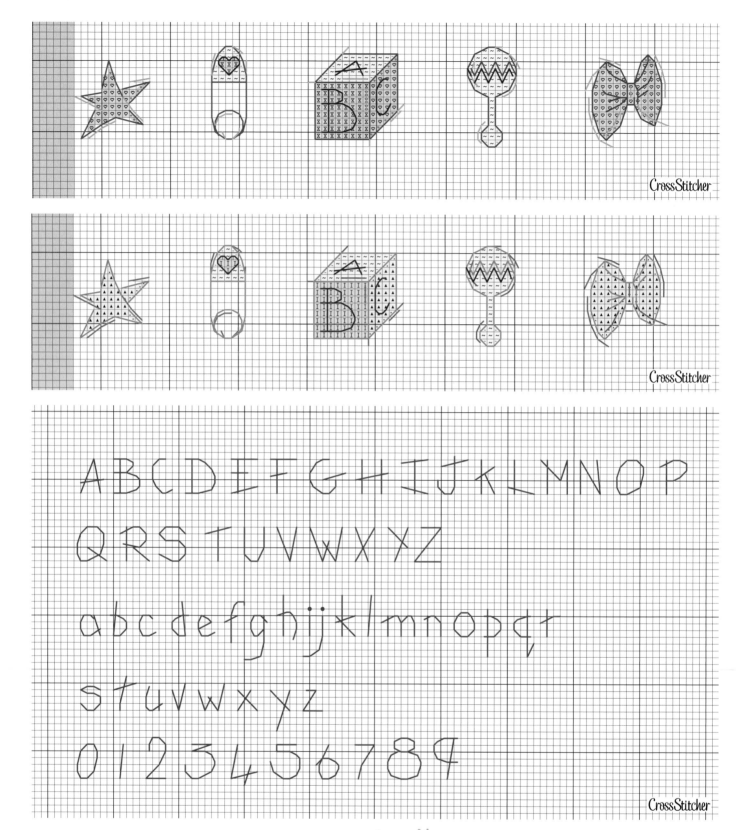

The gray areas on the chart above show the correct spacing between the heart and star motifs – that's nine and a half squares

BASIC BOOTIES

If stitching on ready mades isn't your thing, just attach a pair of ordinary booties to your sampler instead. They're widely available in department stores and baby shops.

CHILDREN

KIDS WILL GO WILD FOR OUR COLLECTION
OF MONSTER BUTTONS AND FUNKY FELTIES,
SO PREPARE TO BE PESTERED!

What a hoot!

This funky owl will jazz up a child's nursery and provide many hours of joy – and we can think of plenty of grown-ups who'd love him too!

Designed by: Lucie Heaton **Stitch time:** 13 hours

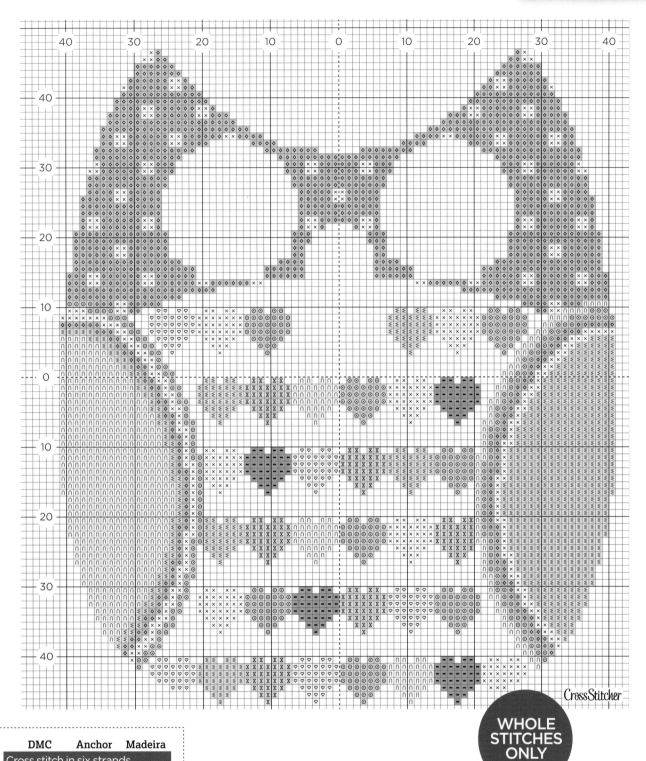

WHOLE
STITCHES
ONLY

	DMC	Anchor	Madeira
Cross stitch in six strands			
✕	White	002	2402
⩘	563	208	1207
✚	602	057	0702
♡	605	1094	0613
◇	741	304	0203
✕	742	303	0114
∩	744	301	0112
⊙	996	433	1103
▬	3860	379	1914

*If you'd rather make
a square cushion instead of a shaped one
with dangly feet, just stick the felt feet
straight on to the aida - easy!*

Templates

Use these shapes to cut out the felt pieces for your owl

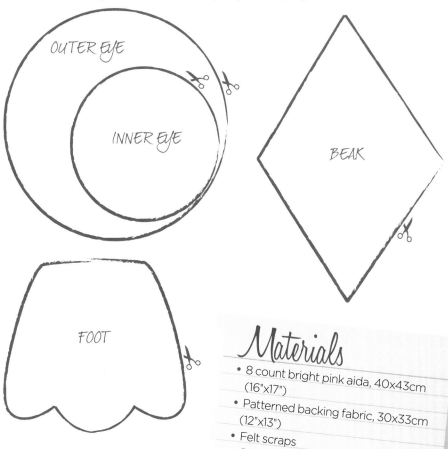

OUTER EYE

INNER EYE

BEAK

FOOT

Materials

- 8 count bright pink aida, 40x43cm (16"x17")
- Patterned backing fabric, 30x33cm (12"x13")
- Felt scraps
- One button
- Stuffing

Make a... cushion

Step 1

TRIM your stitching with 3cm (1¼") of excess all the way round. Cut a piece of backing fabric to the same shape. Cut out felt shapes for the owl's eyes, beak and feet. Use any color felt you like.

Step 2

STITCH two felt 'feet' together. Pin them on the front of your owl. With right sides together, pin your fabric over the top of your owl. Machine stitch around the shape, leaving a gap for turning.

Step 3

TURN right side out. Hand stitch the eyes in place. Attach the small circle to the large one with running stitch. Add a button or stitched curve. Attach using running stitch.

Step 4

ATTACH the beak by stitching through the center of the diamond. Choose a stiff felt. Fold in half and iron over the fold. Finally, stuff the cushion, then slip stitch the gap closed.

Little monsters

Perfect for playground trading, these collectible buttons have definitely got the upper hand on pester power – your kids will love them!

Designed by: Kerry Morgan Stitch time: 1 hour each

Photography by: Neil Godwin

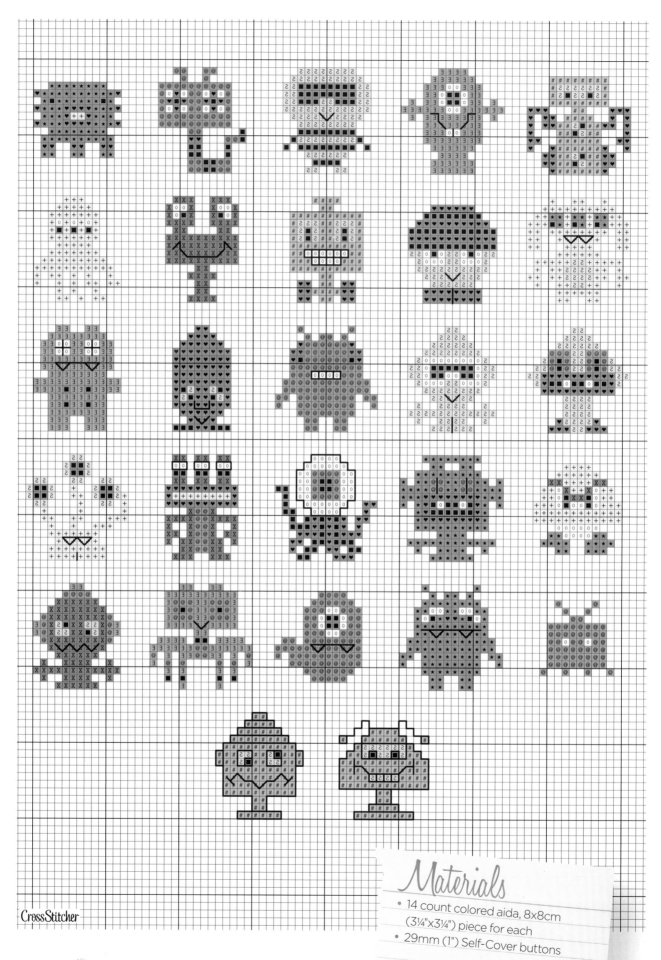

CrossStitcher

Materials

- 14 count colored aida, 8x8cm (3¼"x3¼") piece for each
- 29mm (1") Self-Cover buttons

Make a...
covered button

Step 1

MAKING buttons like these are really quick and easy. Use the template provided on your self-cover button packaging to cut your aida into a circle, with your stitching in the middle.

Step 2

PULL your aida around the button front as tight as you can. We prefer metal self-cover buttons because they have metal teeth to grip your fabric. They are a bit pricier but so much easier to use. It's worth paying the extra!

Step 3

USE your fingernail to tighten and smooth any lumpy areas around the perimeter of your button. Once you're happy with it, pop the backing into place.

	DMC	Anchor	Madeira
Cross stitch in three strands			
0	White	002	2402
■	310	403	2400
#	414	235	1801
+	605	1094	0613
♥	666	046	0210
@	701	227	1305
★	792	941	0905
∃	946	332	0207
X	3803	069	2609
S	3822	295	0112
Backstitch in one strand			
—	310	403	2400
all details			

Buttons are available in both plastic and metal varieties. While the plastic ones are a bit cheaper, the metal ones have teeth that grip the fabric better

Easy as ABC

This sampler is simple enough for a child to stitch, or you could make it for them yourself!

Designed by: Helen Phillips
Stitch time: 15 hours

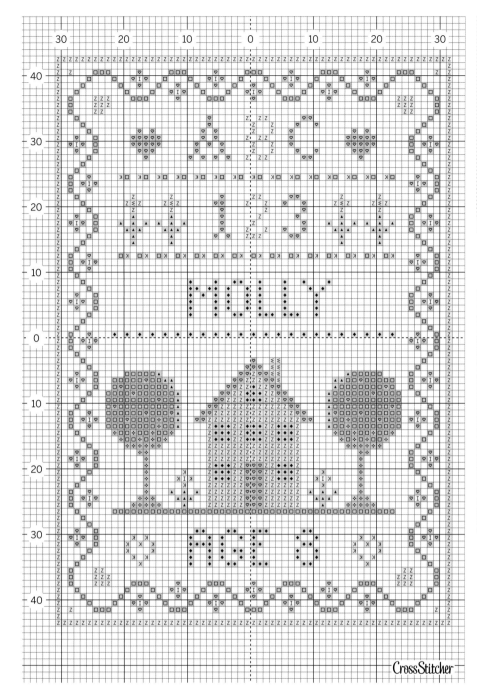

	DMC	Anchor	Madeira
Cross stitch in four strands			
Z	341	117	0901
♥	351	010	0214
✛	436	363	2011
▲	703	238	1307
▢	704	255	1308
I	727	293	0110
◆	793	176	0906
K	3608	086	0709
⊠	3822	295	0112

CrossStitcher

FINDING THE RIGHT FRAME

An embroidery frame or hoop will help you stitch more easily and keep your cross stitches looking neat. If you're using a hoop you will need one that's large enough to hold the whole of your design so that it doesn't squash any stitches. It will also save you having to keep taking the fabric out of the hoop to move it around, which can be distracting as well as causing unsightly marks on your work.

Use the alphabet chart to stitch the name of your choice – have a spare bit of graph paper on hand for plotting the spacing

CrossStitcher

Materials
• 11 count ivory aida, 31x36cm (12¼"x14¼")
• Rustic wood frame

Irresistible Gifts to cross stitch

Animal magic

Both boys and girls will love these quirky accessories. Stitch a few for your kids and all their friends will want some too!

Designed by: Jane Prutton

Stitch time: up to 3 hours each

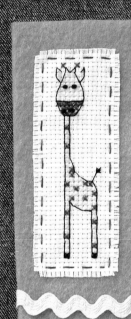

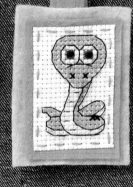
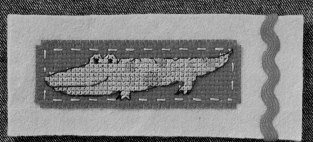

CrossStitcher

Stitch a cute bird on plastic canvas to make a friendship necklace

Homework will be way more fun with a felty giraffe bookmark

Dangle a cheeky little monkey from the zip of your favourite sweater

	DMC	Anchor	Madeira
Cross stitch in two strands			
✕	White	002	2402
▬	155	109	0803
◗	333	119	0903
⧖	433	358	2008
⋉	602	057	0702
♡	604	055	0614
♥	666	046	0210
⊠	738	361	2013
~	739	366	2014
✣	740	316	0202
☆	742	303	0114
⋈	906	256	1411
△	907	255	1410
□	932	1033	1710
⊙	964	185	1112
■	3371	382	2004
⌐	3823	386	2511
Ǝ	3846	1090	1103
Backstitch in two strands			
▬▬	666	046	0210
frog glasses, lips, tongues			
Backstitch in one strand			
▬▬	3371	382	2004
all other outlines and details			
French knots in two strands			
●	3371	382	2004
eyes, giraffe nose			

Make a... covered button

Step 1

MAKING buttons like these are really quick and easy. Use the template provided on your self-cover button packaging to cut your aida into a circle, with your stitching in the middle.

Step 2

PULL your aida around the button front as tight as you can. We prefer metal self-cover buttons because they have metal teeth to grip your fabric. They are a bit pricier but so much easier to use. It's worth paying the extra!

Step 3

USE your fingernail to tighten and smooth any lumpy areas around the perimeter of your button. Once you're happy with it, pop the backing into place.

Materials

- 14 count aida in different colors
- 14 count plastic canvas
- Felt scraps
- Beads, ric rac and cord
- Metal links
- 29mm (1") Self-Cover Buttons

Little rascals!

You won't find these
crafty critters in your wardrobe or under
the bed. Oh no, these are the fun and friendly kind!
Give them to your own little monsters – they'll love them

Designed by: Kerry Morgan **Stitch time:** 9-11 hours each

Turn the page to find out how to make all these wacky gift ideas

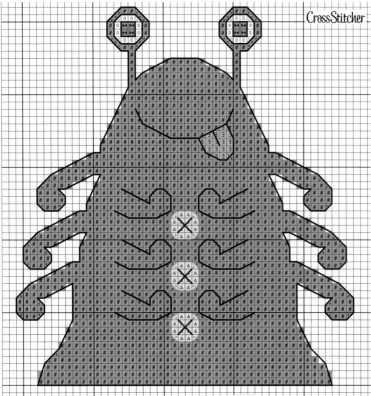

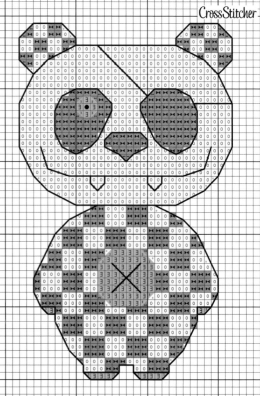

Materials

Padded keyrings

- 14 count pale blue aida, 20x20cm (8"x8") for each
- Felt, 12x12cm (5"x5") piece for each
- Ribbon or felt loop
- Key ring
- Stuffing

Make a... **padded keyring**

Protect your possessions with the help of a few friendly monsters – the more the merrier!

Step 1

DRAW a sewing line on the reverse of your stitching, following the basic shape of the monster. Make the shape as fluid as possible, otherwise it will be difficult to sew accurately.

Step 2

CUT your stitching and a felt piece 1cm (¼") larger than your sewing line. With right sides in, pin in place, sandwiching a ribbon loop at the top. Machine sew, leaving an opening for turning.

Step 3

TURN right side out. Don't worry if it takes a few attempts to get the shape just right. Fill firmly with stuffing and slip stitch the opening closed. Attach your keyring around the ribbon loop.

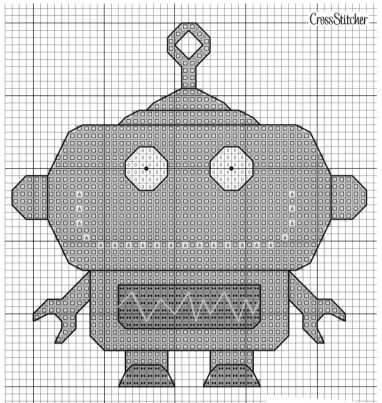

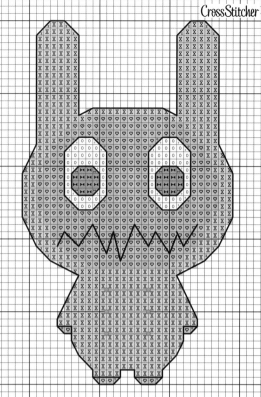

	DMC	Anchor	Madeira
Cross stitch in three strands			
0	White	002	2402
⋈	310	403	2400
□	318	235	1802
#	321	047	0510
△	444	291	0105
♡	972	298	0107
Ɛ	3607	087	0708
X	3846	1090	1105
Backstitch in one strand			
▬	310	403	2400
all other details			
▬	444	291	0105
robot			
▬	972	298	0107
monster			
French knots in two strands			
●	310	403	2400
eyes			
French knots in one strand			
●	972	298	0107
buttons			

PENCIL POT
We used an empty can of pineapple rings for our pencil pot. Remove the label and tap any sharp edges flat with a hammer. Cut your stitching to fit, fray the outer row of aida blocks and attach to your tin with double-sided tape.

Materials

Felt frame
- 14 count white aida, 15x20cm (6"x8")
- Felt, two 18x22cm (7¼"x8¾") pieces in orange and turquoise
- Iron-on interfacing
- Ribbon for hanging

Pencil pot
- 14 count red aida, 20x30cm (8"x12")
- Tin can (ours was a tin of pineapple rings, 11.5cm (4½") tall and 27cm (10¾") around)

Make a…
felt frame
When a traditional frame just won't suit, go for a funky felt version

Step 1
CUT your turquoise felt into an oval. On the reverse, sketch out your scalloped edge and cut out. Now cut an oval aperture into the center measuring 11x14cm (4¼"x5½").

Step 2
CUT an oval aperture in the center of your orange felt, just slightly smaller than the turquoise felt. Now cut scallops around the outside of your orange felt, just slightly larger than the scallops on your turquoise felt.

Step 3
BACK your stitched piece with iron on interfacing. Pin in place behind your felt pieces. Add contrasting straight stitches around the inside edge of the frame. Add running stitch around the outside edge. Finish with a ribbon loop.
See page 37 for photo.

1

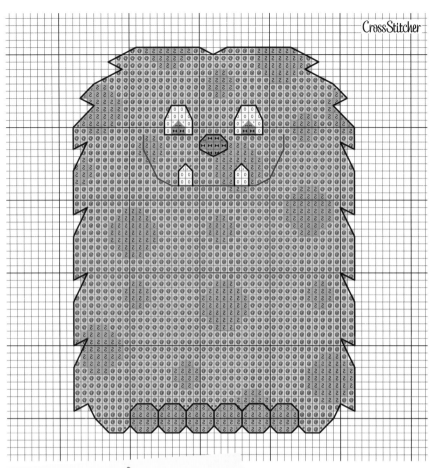

CrossStitcher

DMC	Anchor	Madeira
Cross stitch in three strands		
O White	002	2402
⋈ 310	403	2400
@ 703	238	1307
♥ 972	298	0107
S 995	410	1102
Ɛ 3607	087	0708
Backstitch in one strand		
—— 310	403	2400
all other details		
—— 321	047	0510
mouth		
French knots in two strands		
● 310	403	2400
eyes		

Pick up sheets of felt from any craft or fabric shop.

Materials

Felt book cover
- 14 count white aida, 15x20cm (6"x8")
- Felt, 22.5x44cm (9"x17½")
- Notebook

Make a...**felt book cover**
Swap the sewing machine for hand stitches to create the perfect kid-friendly project

Step 1

CUT a piece of felt to measure 22.5x44cm (9"x17½"). If you're not using an A5 notebook you will need to adjust the size to suit. Trim your stitching to measure about 10x12.5cm (4"x5"). Fray the outer row of aida blocks.

Step 2

LAY your piece of felt on a flat surface. Position your stitched patch in place so the right hand edge is 9cm (3½") from the right hand edge of the felt. Stitch your patch in place using a brightly colored running stitch.

Step 3

MAKE a 6cm (2½") fold toward the reverse on both edges and pin in place. Check your book fits snugly. Using a machine zig zag stitch or a hand running stitch, sew along the top and bottom edges. Finish by popping in your book!

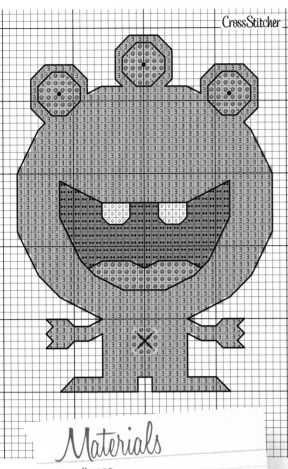

CrossStitcher

Materials

Pencil case

- 14 count yellow aida, 15x20cm (6"x8")
- Striped fabric, three 13x20cm (5¼"x8") pieces
- Iron-on interfacing
- Velcro or metal fasteners

Or try... **this!**

Stitch all six and showcase them in box frames

FRAME all six monsters in dinky box frames to make a wonderfully wacky display for a child's bedroom wall. Pop into your local frame shop to get some custom made.

Make a... **pencil case**

Using Velcro instead of a zip makes this pencil case super quick and easy

Step 1

CUT your stitching to measure 13x20cm (5¼"x8"). Back with iron-on-interfacing. Cut three additional pieces of patterned fabric to the same size.

Step 2

WITH right sides in, sew one patterned piece and your stitching together along the top edge only. Repeat with the other two patterned pieces.

Step 3

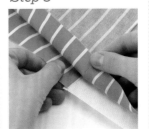

WITH right sides together, line up both sewn pieces so the joins line up. Machine sew all the way around, leaving an opening for turning on the lining side.

Step 4

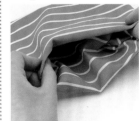

TURN right side out and slip stitch the opening closed. Push the lining inside. Press the folds flat. Add Velcro or metal fasteners to finish.

The fox & the gingerbread man

Recreate the classic fairytale in cross stitch with some fun decorations that look good enough to eat!

Designed by: Anette Eriksson
Stitch time: up to 5 hours each

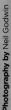

We cut out every other pompom on our shelf-edging trim to create a more subtle look

Use any trim you like to finish your shelf-edging. We've gone for two classics – ric rac and pompoms!

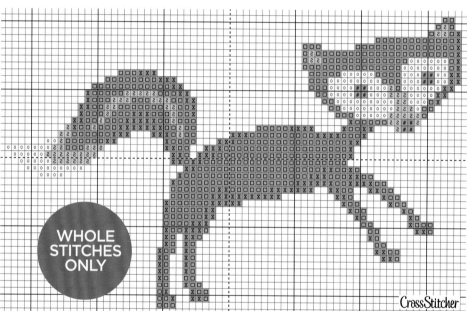

WHOLE STITCHES ONLY

CrossStitcher

SPACING

Leave about 5.5-6cm (2"-2½") between the end of one design and the beginning of the next. This will create a finished design length of approximately 65cm (25½"). If you're stitching on a 1m (1 yard) length of aida band, begin stitching the fox about 18cm (7") from the left-hand edge and your design will be centerd.

Materials

Shelf edging
- 10cm (4") wide white aida band, 1m (1 yard)
- Chunky cream ric rac, 1m (1 yard)
- Small bobble trim, 1m (1 yard)
- White backing fabric, 12x100cm (4¾"x39")

Picture
- White frame, 15x20cm (6"x8")
- White mount with 10x15cm (4"x6") aperture
- Chunky cream cord, 38cm (15")

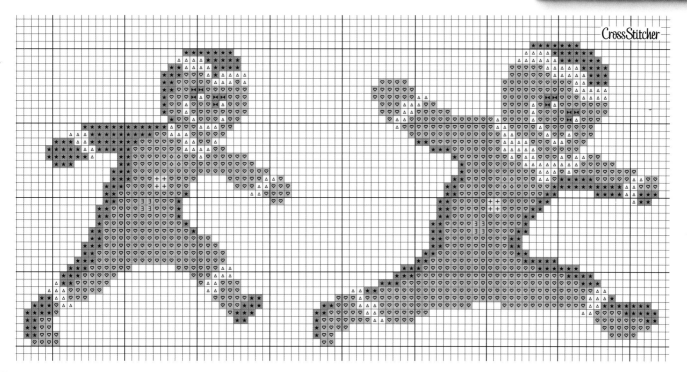

DMC	Anchor	Madeira
Cross stitch in two strands		
+ 165	278	1414
⋈ 310	403	2400
★ 433	358	2008
♡ 435	365	2010
Ǝ 553	098	0712
◇ 602	057	0702
△ 712	926	2101
○ 746	275	0101
☒ 919	340	0313
□ 920	1004	0312
ς 922	1003	0310
# 3799	868	1713

Make…
shelf edging

Step 1
FOLD the cut edges of your aida band under and machine stitch in place. Fold the edges of your white backing fabric under, creating a strip that's 9.5cm (3¾") wide and the same length as your aida band. Press flat with an iron.

Step 2
WITH right sides facing out, pin and machine stitch in place on the reverse of your aida band. Using small tacking stitches attach ric rac along the top edge of your aida band. Attach ric rac to the bottom edge.

Why not replace the gingerbread men's buttons with real ones? Try tiny ones in different colors

Oh boy!

Turn these cool cartoons into fun
birthday cards for boys

Designed by: Jenny Barton Stitch time: 8 hours each

DMC	Anchor	Madeira
Cross stitch in three strands		
✕ White	002	2402
■ 310	403	2400
◐ 553	098	0712
♥ 666	046	0210
▲ 703	238	1307
✕ 725	305	0108
⋒ 738	361	2013
♡ 760	1022	0405
ⱪ 793	176	0906
◪ 841	1082	1911
⌐ 950	4146	2309
Backstitch in one strand		
— 413	236	1713
all other details		
— 666	046	0210
lettering		
— 740	316	0202
lettering		
— 793	176	0906
lettering		

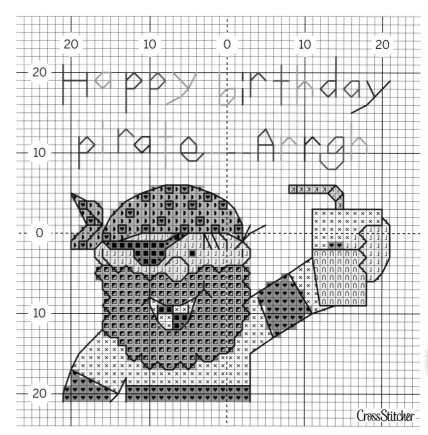

Make a... card

Step 1

BEGIN by cutting a 12x24cm (4¾"x9½") piece of corrugated card. To create the fold, measure and mark the center on the smooth side of the card. Lightly score with a craft knife, taking care not to actually cut through.

Step 2

IF YOUR corrugated card came on a roll, it might be difficult to work with at first. Once you've cut your card, press it flat under a heavy book for a while until the card lies flat.

Step 3

USE a glue stick to attach your stitching to a piece of white card. Cut around the design. Attach to the center of your corrugated card using double-sided tape or 3D foam pads.

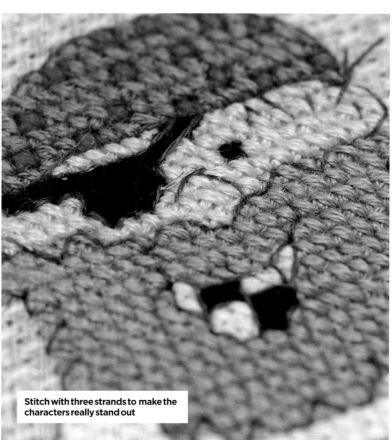

Stitch with three strands to make the characters really stand out

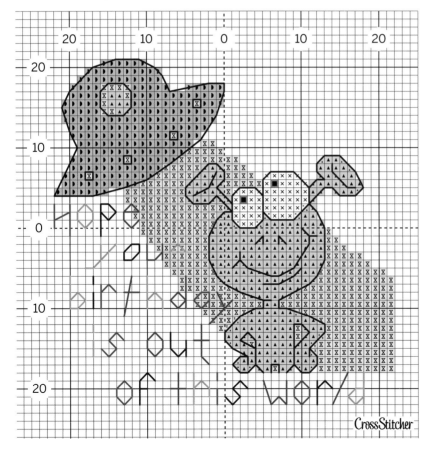

In a hurry? Save yourself a bit of time by stitching the lettering in just one thread shade instead of making them different colors like we've done. The multicolored effect is really funky, but it can be fiddly to keep changing threads!

RUSTIC AIDA

Rustic aida has a slightly stiffer texture than regular aida. This makes it a more forgiving choice for beginner stitchers, as variations in stitching tension will be less likely to show, especially with brightly colored designs like these cards. Make sure you stitch using three strands instead of two for the best effect and coverage

Materials
- 14 count 18x18cm (7"x7") rustic aida
- Corrugated card
- White card to back your design

ROMANCE

EVERYTHING YOU NEED FOR WEDDINGS,
ANNIVERSARIES AND VALENTINE'S DAY, OR JUST
A ROMANTIC TREAT FOR YOUR OTHER HALF

Fit for a king

How do we like our eggs in the morning?
Scrambled? Fried? No, it's boiled with
a royal egg cozy of course!

Designed by: Diane Machin Stitch time: 5 hours each

Photography by Neil Godwin

Materials

- 28 count purple evenweave, two 15x18cm (6"x7") pieces for each
- Purple lining fabric, 11x13cm (4½"x5¼")
- Mini red pompoms
- Gold ric rac, 12cm (5")
- Purple ribbon, 12cm (5")

	DMC	Anchor	Madeira
Cross stitch in two strands			
Ǝ	DMC Light Effects E677		
@	DMC Light Effects E703		
♥	DMC Light Effects E815		
5	DMC Light Effects E3821		
★	DMC Light Effects E3837		
Backstitch in two strands			
——	550	101	0714

all details

Backstitch in two strands of cotton and one strand metallic			
——	550	101	0714

DMC Light Effects E3821 lettering

METALLICS

Metallic threads can get tangled very easily. Make things easier by coating your threads in beeswax or a thread conditioner such as Thread Heaven before you begin stitching. Thread Heaven is available at most sewing shops.

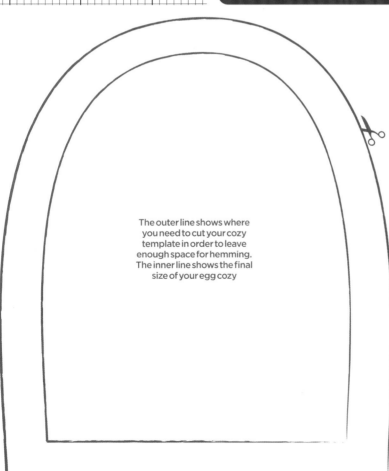

The outer line shows where you need to cut your cozy template in order to leave enough space for hemming. The inner line shows the final size of your egg cozy

Make an… egg cozy

Step 1

FIRST cut out and trace the cozy template below on to the back of your stitching. Cut a second piece of purple evenweave plus two pieces of purple lining fabric using the same template.

Step 2

WITH right sides in, machine stitch one lining and one evenweave piece together along the straight edge only. Open and press the seam flat with an iron. Repeat with your second set of evenweave and lining. Machine stitch your ribbon and ric rac along the bottom edges of each evenweave piece.

Step 3

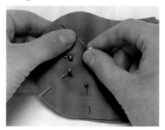

WITH right sides in, machine stitch all the way around the shape, leaving an opening for turning on the unstitched side. Be sure your seams line up in the middle. Turn right side out, slip stitch closed and push the lining inside. Finish with a mini red pompom on top.

Sent with love...

These chic hearts are perfect for jazzing up gifts for
Valentine's Day, weddings or just a treat for a loved one

Designed by: Angela Poole
Stitch time: 1-2 hours each

TEA FOR TWO

GIVE a tea-lover a thoughtful present with
tins accompanied by a floral
love-heart gift tag
Loose leaf teas, *Whittards*

TEEN STYLE

POP some luxurious body cream in
a handmade bag finished with a trendy
Union Jack stitched heart
Body cream, *Marks and Spencer*

BUDDING BLOOMS

PRESENT a simple bud vase in style with this
sweetheart gift tag. For added passion include
a few long-stemmed roses
Pink heart bud vase, *Marks and Spencer*

LIGHT EFFECT

DAINTY and elegant, this tealight holder
just needs a handmade gift tag to finish it off
Glass tea light holder,
Marks and Spencer

WRITE UP

TURN a plain luggage label into a stitched
gift tag for this travel-themed writing paper
Trudy Travels Writing Paper,
Accessorize

LOVE NOTES

PAIR this girly pen with some earrings in a small
bag tied with string for a romantic surprise
Ball pen, *Waterstones*
Earrings, *Accessorize*

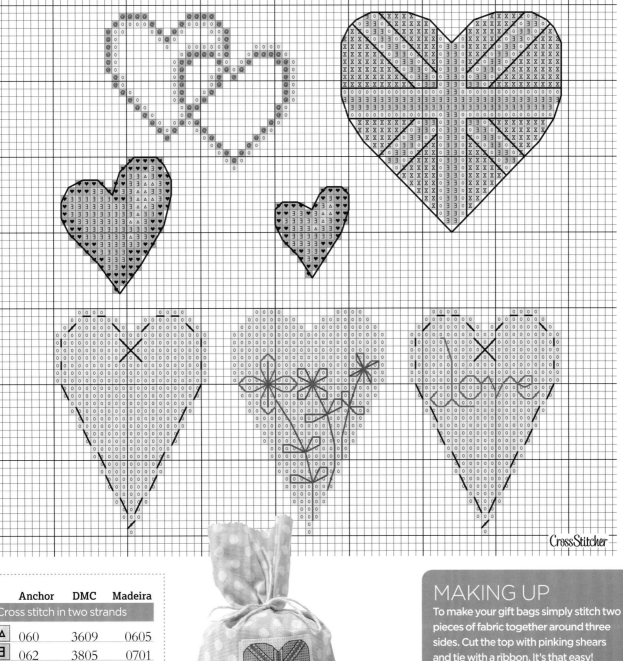

	Anchor	DMC	Madeira
Cross stitch in two strands			
△	060	3609	0605
Ǝ	062	3805	0701
♥	063	601	0702
✗	167	3766	1111
@	168	807	1108
0	387	Ecru	2314
Backstitch in one strand			
——	062	3805	0701
flowers, lettering, star			
——	097	554	0711
flowers			
——	169	3760	2506
leaves, stem			
——	401	413	1713
all other details			

MAKING UP

To make your gift bags simply stitch two pieces of fabric together around three sides. Cut the top with pinking shears and tie with a ribbon. It's that easy! Create the gift tags by sticking a patch of pinking sheared fabric to a paper gift tag. Cut out and attach your stitching using 3D foam pads for a raised effect.

These projects use a variety of materials including aida, perforated paper, patterned fabric, ribbon and gift tags.

I ♥ U forever

Tell someone how you feel with one of these gorgeous little buttons, complete with cute and quirky sentiments. Choose your favorites and get stitching!

Designed by: Kerry Morgan
Stitch time: 2 hours each

Work the cross stitch in three strands and the backstitch in two for an extra bold look

CrossStitcher

Jazz up a store-bought purse with a single cute button

Affix a bit of elastic or cord to make a funky phone charm

Forget store-bought cards – a single button and some pretty fabric is all you need

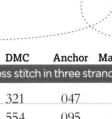

	DMC	Anchor	Madeira
Cross stitch in three strands			
⋈	321	047	0510
♡	554	095	0711
ƨ	597	1064	1110
◆	601	063	0703
△	743	305	0113
0	745	300	0111
▲	807	168	1108
♥	891	035	0411
#	907	255	1410
Ǝ	966	240	1209
@	993	1070	1201
+	3354	074	2610
☒	3819	278	2703
★	3837	111	0713
Backstitch in two strands			
——	154	070	0714
lettering			
——	3371	382	2004
lettering			
——	3799	236	1713
lettering			

Materials

- 14 count white aida, 10x10cm (4"x4") piece for each button
- 29mm (1") Self-Cover buttons

Make a... covered button

Step 1

MAKING buttons like these are really quick and easy. Use the template provided on your self-cover button packaging to cut your aida into a circle, with your stitching in the middle.

Step 2

PULL your aida around the button front as tight as you can. We prefer metal self-cover buttons because they have metal teeth to grip your fabric. They are a bit pricier but so much easier to use. It's worth paying the extra!

Step 3

USE your fingernail to tighten and smooth any lumpy areas around the perimeter of your button. Once you're happy with it, pop the backing into place.

Top tip!

Cut a circle out of fabric, add a running stitch around the outside edge and pull the thread ends to create a rosette.

Wedding bells

Cross stitch meets beading in this beautifully intricate sampler – and it's so versatile you could make it for a wedding or anniversary

Having a really lovely adaptable wedding design on hand is a must for every stitcher who likes to stitch for special occasions. Whether you're making an engagement present, memento of the big day itself, or celebrating 50 years of marriage, this design can be revamped and stitched again and again. Substitute the gold thread for the bride's scheme shade, or go for sparkling red for a ruby anniversary. The possibilities are endless, and all you need is a bit of imagination to get the result you want.

Designed by: Lesley Teare
Design size: 16x17cm (6¼"x6¾")
Stitch time: 30 hours

Or try... **this!**

Short on time? Stitch the smaller design and turn it into a patch for a wedding album

Materials

Frame
- 28 count evenweave, 32x32cm (13"x13")
- Seed beads
- White box frame

Photography by Neil Godwin

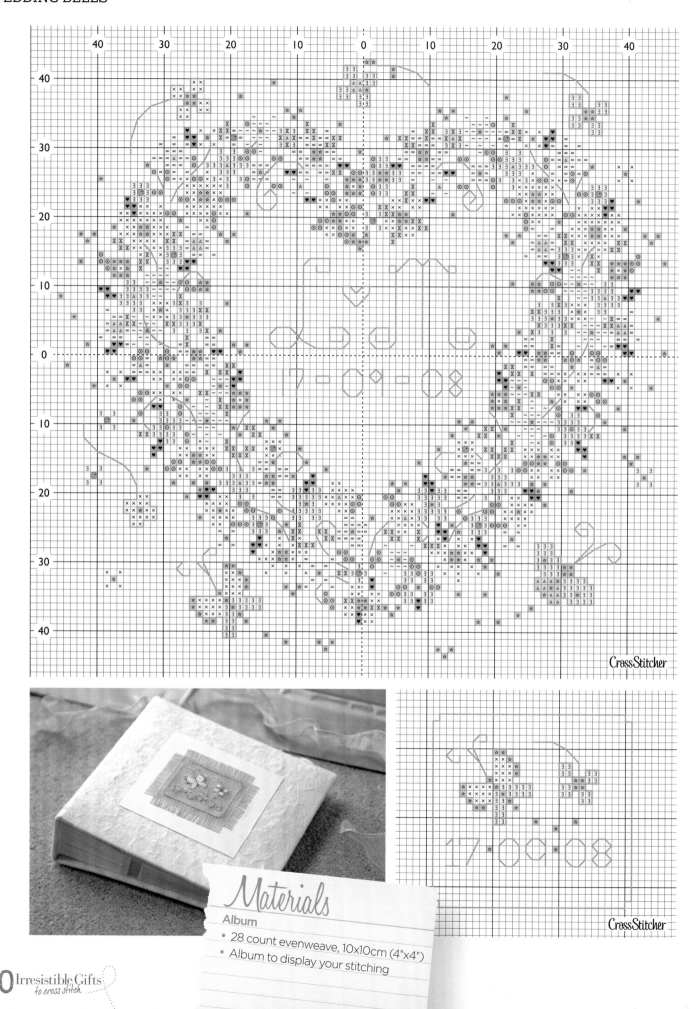

Materials

Album
- 28 count evenweave, 10x10cm (4"x4")
- Album to display your stitching

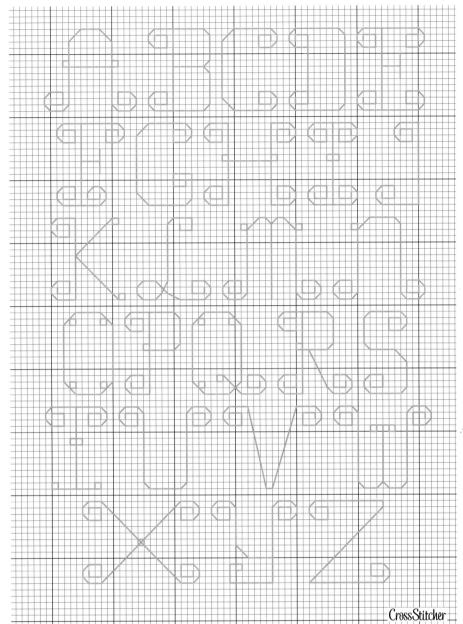

	DMC	Anchor	Madeira
Cross stitch in two strands			
✕	B5200	001	2401
⊙	471	265	1501
=	746	275	0101
△	3046	887	2206
♥	3346	267	1407
✕	3348	264	1409
ⅎ	3823	386	2512
~	3865	926	2402
☆	DMC Light Effects 3852		
Backstitch in one strand			
—	DMC Light Effects E3852 *all outlines and details*		
Attach beads with cotton			
●	Mill Hill seed beads 00557 *flowers*		

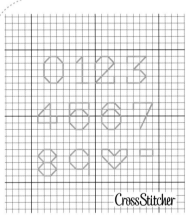

How to... add beads

Step 1

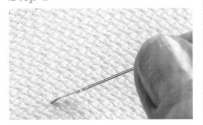

THREAD your beading needle, or a size 9 or 10 embroidery needle, with one strand of cotton. Strengthen it by running it over a tablet of beeswax or a thread conditioner.

Step 2

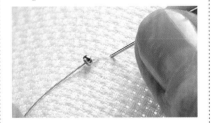

SECURE your thread on the reverse and bring your needle to the front. Thread on the bead and make a diagonal half cross stitch over one aida block or two evenweave threads.

Step 3

BEADS can be added singly or in clusters as shown here. Always keep your thread taut. To finish your thread, weave it through the reverse of your stitches.

Perfect pair

Make these gorgeous folksy motifs into fun gatefold cards for Valentine's Day

Designed by: Jenny Barton
Stitch time: 8 hours each

Materials

- 14 count aida, two 15x15cm (6"x6") pieces for each card
- White gatefold cards
- White card to back your designs
- White 3D foam pads
- Thin red ribbon

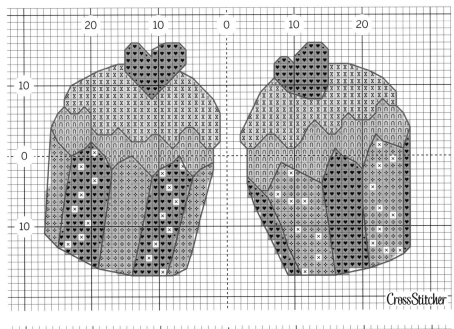

	DMC	Anchor	Madeira
Cross stitch in two strands			
✗ White	002		2402
Z	519	1038	1105
✗	743	302	0113
✤	807	168	1108
♡	3706	033	0409
■	3799	236	1713
♥	3801	1098	0411
▲	3849	1070	1109
∩	3854	313	2301
Backstitch in one strand			
—— White	002		2402
eye			
——	3799	236	1713
all other details			

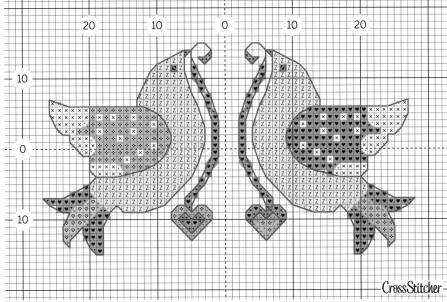

Make a...
gatefold card

Step 1

ONCE you've finished stitching, turn to the reverse and iron. Before you trim your stitching use a glue stick to attach it to a piece of white card. Now carefully trim around each shape, leaving a border of one aida block.

Step 2

ATTACH one stitched shape to each side of your gatefold card using white 3D foam pads. We've chosen 3mm (⅛") foam pads for our cards, but they're also available in 2mm (1⁄16") and 1mm (1⁄32") varieties if you'd like a slightly more subtle 3D effect.

Step 3

ATTACH your ribbon to the inside of each card. Alternatively you could punch a small hole into each side of your cards and loop the ribbon ends through the holes. Attach the ribbon on the cherry card so it lines up with the stems. For the bird card, attach the ribbon either at the birds' beaks or in the center. For the cupcake card, simply attach in the middle of the card.

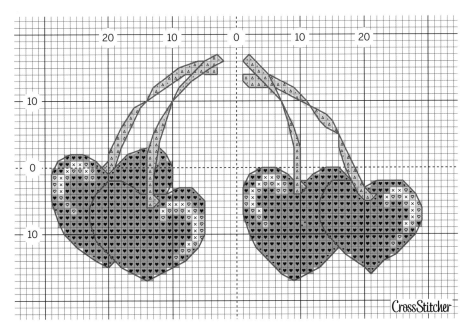

Say it...
with stitching

This quick and simple heart sachet makes
a brilliant gift for Valentine's Day

Designed by: Brenda Keyes

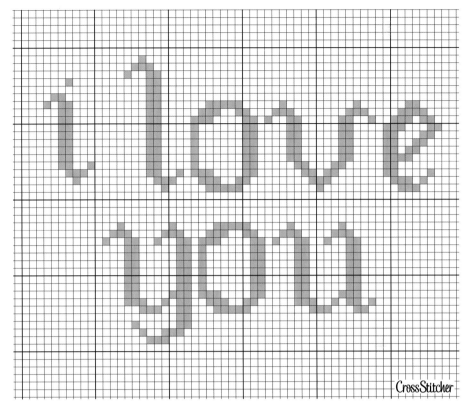

Cross Stitcher

Stitch it on aida!
If you'd rather not stitch on linen, choose a 14 count aida instead.

Linen fabric is much easier to work with when you're making sachets, because it's softer and finer than aida. You'll find it gives a much smoother finish!

Materials

- 28 count linen, 18x18cm (7¼"x7¼") piece
- Ribbon for hanging
- Stuffing

Make a... **heart sachet**
Two easy steps to a polished, professional finish

Step 1

CUT a basic heart template out of card. Use the template to trace and cut out your stitching and a piece of backing fabric.

Step 2

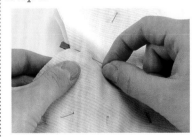

WITH right sides in, sew your heart shapes together, sandwiching a ribbon in between. Leave an opening for turning. Slip stitch closed to finish.

Fill it with... **roses**

TRY filling your heart sachet with potpourri or dried rose buds. And remember, presentation matters! Pack the finished heart in tissue paper and wrap it up in a box with ribbon. Gorgeous!

True love

Want something a bit alternative? Try this funky purse in Emily Peacock's trademark style

Designed by: Emily Peacock
Stitch time: 10 hours

Materials

- 14 count cream aida 18x22cm (7¼"x8¾")
- Red backing fabric 18x22cm (7¼"x8¾")
- Iron-on interfacing
- 16cm (6") zipper
- Heart charm

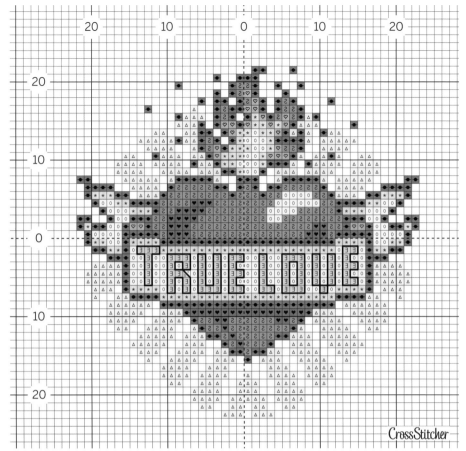

DMC	Anchor	Madeira
Cross stitch in two strands		
321	047	0510
743	302	0113
747	158	1104
809	130	0909
814	045	0514
970	925	0204
3750	1036	1712
3865	926	2402
Backstitch in one strand		
3750	1036	1712
all details		

Love this design? Visit www.emilypeacock.com for more great projects by Emily

Add a bit of sparkle by stitching the heart in DMC's Light Effects thread.

Make a...
purse

Step 1
BACK your design with iron-on interfacing. Tack the finished dimensions of the purse around the design – our purse measures 12x16cm (4¾"x6").

Step 2
PLACE the zipper face down along your top tacking line and pin and machine stitch in place.

Step 3
NOW stitch your backing fabric to the other side of the zipper. Place both pieces of fabric right sides together and machine stitch along the remaining three sides using your tacking line as a guide.

Step 4
THE final step is to open the zipper and turn the purse right side out. Add your heart charm to the end of the zipper and that's all there is to it.

LOVED ONES

FROM MOTHER'S DAY AND BIRTHDAYS TO
GIFTS FOR TEACHERS – THERE'S SOMETHING
FOR EVERYONE AND EVERY OCCASION HERE!

Funky teatime

What does every mom like? A nice cup of tea, of course! And your mom will love this jazzy handmade tea cozy as a Mother's Day gift this year

❖❖❖❖❖❖❖❖❖❖❖❖❖❖❖❖❖❖❖❖❖❖❖❖❖❖❖❖❖❖❖❖

Designed by: Emily Peacock Stitch time: 30 hours

Materials

- 25 count evenweave, 33x33cm (13"x13")
- Patterned fabric, 27x30cm (10¾"x12")
- Contrasting fabric, 6x55cm (2½"x22") strip
- Lining fabric, two 27x30cm (10¾"x12") pieces
- Wadding, two 27x30cm (10¾"x12") pieces
- Chunky pink ric rac, 1m (1 yard)

Photography by Philip Sowels **Vintage china supplied by** Mrs Stokes www.mrsstokes.com

WHOLE STITCHES ONLY

Customize the design to suit your taste by playing with the colors and patterns a bit. For instance, we stitched the lettering on the tea cozy in just one thread shade instead of in stripes

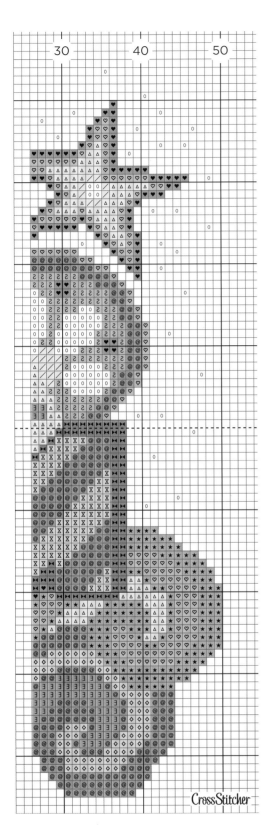

CrossStitcher

DMC	Anchor	Madeira
Cross stitch in three strands		
o White	002	2402
∩ 445	288	0103
★ 552	099	0713
♥ 602	057	0702
@ 700	228	1304
◇ 742	303	0114
∃ 817	013	0211
⊠ 907	255	1410
♥ 917	089	0706
S 947	330	0205
/ 973	290	0105
△ 3708	031	0408
◄ 3777	1015	2502

Stitch it on aida!
You can stitch your design on 14 count gray or yellow aida instead.

Make a... tea cozy

With this zingy accessory in pride of place on the table, afternoon tea will never be dull again!

Step 1

CUT two pieces of patterned fabric, two lining, and two wadding into half circles. Cut your design to an oval. Sew onto one of your fabric pieces and add ric rac.

Step 2

WITH right sides out, sandwich one piece of wadding between your stitched piece and a lining piece. Repeat with the second pieces of fabric, lining and wadding.

Step 3

WITH right sides in, pin and stitch the two sets of fabric together, just around the curved edge. Sandwich ric rac between the layers and a fabric tab at the top.

Step 4

FOLD both edges of your fabric strip under and press in place. Now fold the entire strip in half and press again. Wrap around the raw fabric edges and stitch in place.

QUICK STITCH

For a quick alternative, pick up a funky ready made tea cozy. Add your design as a patch and add chunky ric rac just like we did for the perfect finishing touch. No one will know you didn't sew it all yourself!

A Spanish welcome

Need a housewarming present? This gorgeously eye-popping door sign
will give guests a lovely welcome, Mediterranean style

Designed by: Emily Peacock

Stitch time: 25 hours

Materials

- 14 count aida, 30x35cm (12"x14")
- Wooden frame
- Red cord, 50cm (20")

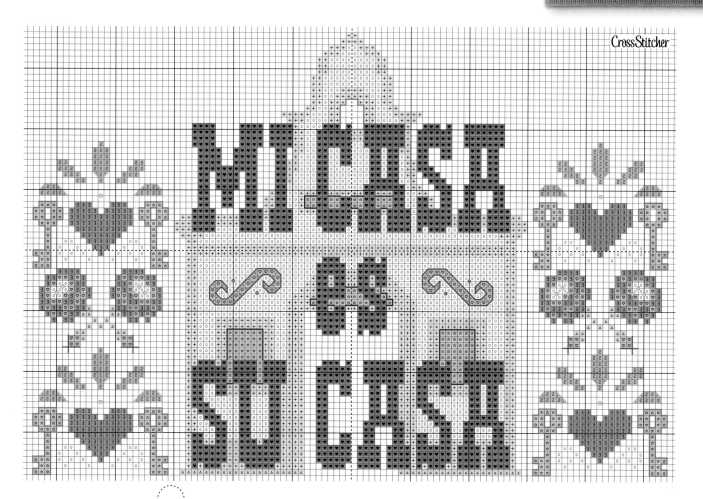

CrossStitcher

DMC	Anchor	Madeira
Cross stitch in three strands		
O White	002	2402
∃ 321	047	0510
★ 422	372	2102
S 553	098	0712
+ 725	305	0108
△ 907	255	1410
♡ 956	040	0611
♥ 3777	1015	2502
Backstitch in one strand		
___ 321	047	0510
all other details		
___ 3777	1015	2502
windows, door		
___ 3828	373	2103
keys, bell tower		
French knots in two strands		
● 553	098	0712
swirls		
● 725	305	0108
flower centers		

Make a... **canvas mount**

Step 1

CUT a piece of mount card to the same size as a basic frame and attach to the front. Mark the center points along the frame and fabric edges.

Step 2

PLACE some carpet tape to the reverse of the frame. Match up the center points of fabric and frame using measurements made in Step 1.

Step 3

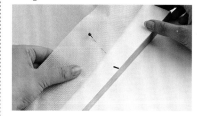

STRETCH the fabric tightly over your frame edge. Fold along the same fabric grain to keep the fabric square. Fold the fabric at each of the four corners.

Step 4

STAPLE the fabric to the reverse and trim excess fabric. Staple the cord in place. Secure any fabric edges on the reverse with strips of masking tape.

Daddy cool!

Tall, short, dark or blonde – we've got a button badge for every kind of dad. Surprise him on Father's Day with a piece of your handiwork

Designed by: Julia Rigby

Stitch time: 3 hours each

	Anchor	DMC	Madeira
Cross stitch in two strands			
~	002	White	2402
Ǝ	013	349	0211
@	098	553	0712
☆	140	3755	0910
♥	142	322	0911
X	255	907	1410
%	256	906	1411
=	293	727	0110
♡	324	721	0308
◆	326	720	0309
□	349	3776	2306
O	366	739	2013
#	378	3863	2601
◘	382	3371	2004
ς	399	318	1802
+	885	Ecru	2014
▲	936	632	2311
/	1010	951	2308
∩	1011	948	2314
△	1020	3713	0808
◇	1021	761	0404
&	1045	436	2011
★	1050	3781	1913
Backstitch in one strand			
——	381	938	2006
all other details			
French knots in one strand			
●	381	938	2006
shirt, eyes, earring			

CrossStitcher

Have a go at mixing and matching colors and elements to create a design that looks just like your own dad

Materials

- 29mm (1") Self-Cover buttons
- 18 count white aida, 10x10cm (4"x4") piece for each button

Moms rule!

Choose one of these funky button designs to put
a smile on your mom's face on Mother's Day – or stitch
one for your sister or best friend instead

Designed by: Julia Rigby

Stitch time: 3 hours each

*It's a cinch to swap any
of the thread colors to
create a button that looks
just like your mom*

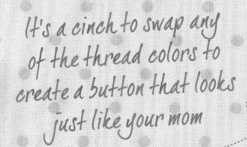

	Anchor	DMC	Madeira
Cross stitch in two strands			
×	002	White	2402
♥	013	817	0211
Ǝ	020	816	2502
/	048	818	0608
▲	110	208	2710
X	140	3755	0910
#	142	322	0911
@	238	703	1306
▶◀	258	904	1413
▵	293	727	0110
ꙅ	339	3830	0312
ꓷ	362	437	2012
o	366	739	2013
I	376	3864	1910
>	378	3863	2601
★	382	3371	2004
□	400	317	1714
∩	885	Ecru	2014
♥	936	632	2311
~	1010	951	2314
*	1011	948	2308
+	1020	3713	0808
2	1021	761	0404
◇	1046	435	2010
◆	1050	3781	1913
Backstitch in two strands			
—	013	817	0211
—	142	322	0911
Backstitch in one strand			
—	381	938	2301
French knots in one strand			
●	013	817	0211
●	142	322	0911
●	238	703	1306
●	381	938	2301
Attach with cotton			
⊙		Size 11 seed beads	
◉		Seed bead on sequin	

CrossStitcher

Don't worry if you've never used 18 count aida before. As long as you have a good craft light you'll be fine!

Materials
- 18 count white aida, 10x10cm (4"x4") piece for each
- 29mm (1") Self-Cover Buttons
- Seed beads and sequins

Irresistible Gifts to cross stitch

Trick or treat

Prepare to be pestered by the kids in the run-up to Halloween. These goodies are so seriously spooky you're just going to have to stitch them all. Sorry.

Designed by: Jenny Barton
Stitch time: up to 4 hours each

Photography by Joby Sessions

Materials

- 14 count plastic canvas
- Ribbons and bamboo skewers
- Square cards

Irresistible Gifts
to cross stitch

DMC	Anchor	Madeira
Cross stitch in two strands		
✕ White	002	2402
↓ 307	289	0104
■ 310	403	2400
◢ 317	400	1714
◇ 372	887	2110
▬ 414	235	1801
◗ 552	099	0713
I 554	095	0711
∩ 640	393	1905
S 642	392	1903
♥ 666	9046	0210
K 741	304	0203
★ 742	303	0114
O 793	176	0906
8 906	256	1411
◉ 931	1034	1711
2 973	290	0105
≤ 3041	871	0806
Z DMC Glow-in-the-Dark		E940
Backstitch in one strand		
▬▬ 310	403	2400
all other details		
▬▬ 976	1001	2302
pumpkins		

Stick a little magnetic strip onto the back of each of your motifs to make spooky fridge magnets!

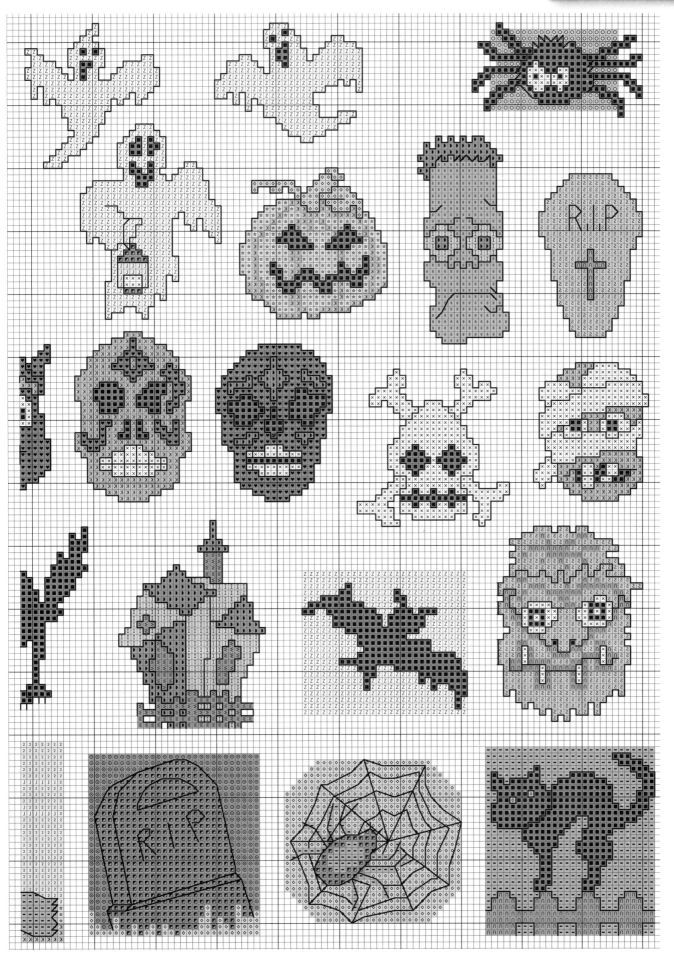

Bits and bobs

Treat a fellow stitcher to this crafty gift set that takes just a couple of evenings to make

Designed by: Debbie Cripps

Stitch time: 3 hours each

a stitch
in time

I ♥ cross stitch!

Buttons

Materials

- 14 count antique white aida, 15x15cm (6"x6") for each design
- Mini buttons
- Scissors charm
- Green aperture card
- Aperture box
- Aperture hanger

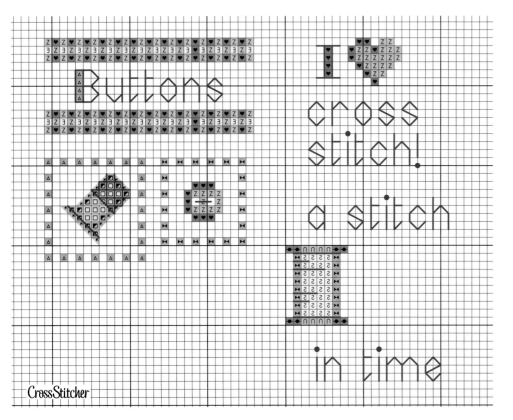

CrossStitcher

How to use a...
waste knot

Step 1

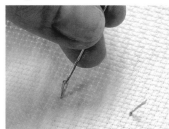

THE waste knot is used to start off a thread in a way that will secure it on the back. Knot one end of your thread and take it through the fabric, about 2cm (¾") from your starting point. Bring it back to the surface to make your first stitch.

Step 2

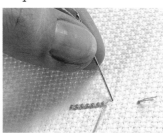

NEXT, work a row of cross stitches towards your knot, or alternatively work a row of half crosses (/ / /) and then work back along the same row to finish the cross (\ \ \ ).

Step 3

A WASTE knot will secure your starting thread on the reverse of your work, as shown here. Once you're happy your thread is secure simply snip the knot off with a sharp pair of scissors.

TIMESAVER
Stitch small designs onto a large piece of fabric then cut each design out and frame. This is quicker and less fiddly than working on several smaller pieces of fabric.

Secure the scissors charm with a stitch on the handle and another on the middle of the scissors – easy!

	Anchor	DMC	Madeira
Cross stitch in two strands			
Ǝ	006	353	0304
Z	010	351	0214
♥	020	498	0511
⌐	144	800	0908
△	215	320	1311
∩	943	422	2102
●	944	869	2105
⋈	978	322	1004
Backstitch in one strand			
—	1041	844	1810
all details			
French knots in one strand			
●	1041	844	1810
lettering			

To save even more time try using DMC's Color Variations thread for the borders

Easter Egg-stravaganza

Give your home the full Easter treatment this year with gorgeous handstitched bunting, pretty gift bags and fun decorations for your tea table. Just add simnel cake and lots of chocolate eggs – yum!

Designed by: Margaret Sherry

Even though we all moan about it from time to time, we secretly love the fun of preparing for Christmas – so why is it we never get our needles out for Easter in the same way? After all, the light is better for stitching, there are loads of gorgeous springy colors to choose from, and the very talented Margaret Sherry has designed a whole set of chicks and bunnies for you to turn into a spectacular Easter display for your home.

Turn the page for all the charts and instructions – it's really easy, promise!

Photography by Neil Godwin

Back your cake band with iron-on interfacing to keep it looking fresh and white. Finish by hemming the cut edges under for a neat finish

Materials

Cake band
- 7.6cm (3") white aida band, 80cm (32")
- Iron-on interfacing

Materials

Cards
- Brown card, 11x20cm (4"x7") for small card, 17x22cm (6"x8") for large card, folded in half

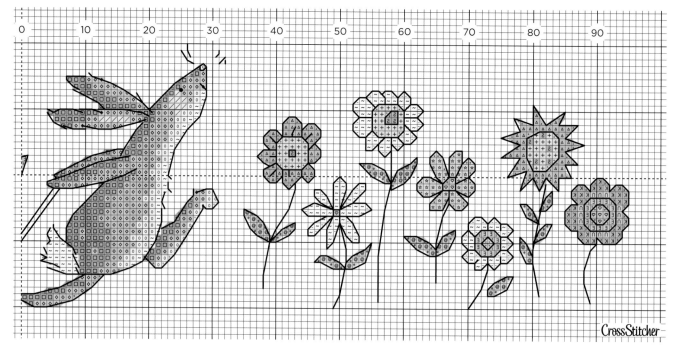

Anchor

Cross stitch in two strands

~	002	⋈	243
/	006	0	275
△	055	+	293
♥	057	♡	305
★	108	ꙅ	314
⋝	109	□	362
∩	120	◇	942
Ƙ	140	▲	1013
◆	146	★	1030
⊠	185	×	1092
#	187	Ǝ	1094
@	241		

Backstitch in two strands

— 314
chicks

Backstitch in one strand

— 236
all other details

French knots in one strand

● 236
eyes

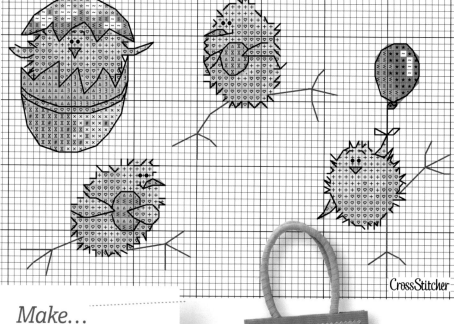

Make...
gift bags

A fun and crafty way to deliver your Easter eggs this year!

TO MAKE your gift bags, first back your stitching with iron-on adhesive and cut out using pinking shears. Fuse to a piece of patterned fabric. Back the fabric with iron-on interfacing and cut out. Attach to your bag using double-sided tape.
For a finishing touch, wrap your bag handles with cotton ribbon like we've done.

Materials

Gift bags
• Small paper gift bags
• Cotton ribbon to wrap handles
• Patterned fabrics
• Iron-on adhesive
• Iron-on-interfacing

Cross Stitcher

Make...felt decorations

Hang them on some bare branches from your garden

Step 1

BACK your stitching with iron-on adhesive. Sketch an egg shape and cut out using pinking shears.

Step 2

FUSE your stitching to a piece of felt. If your felt is particularly thin you might want to fuse two pieces together. Cut out, about 5mm (2") beyond your stitched shape.

Step 3

ATTACH a ribbon loop to the back of your felt. If you like, thread a few glass beads onto the loop.

FUN WITH FABRICS

These little projects are perfect for using up old scraps of fabric and ribbons lying around in your stash. To get the classic Easter look, choose a mixture of plain and patterned fabrics in nice pastel colors – stripes and polka dots are ideal. If you haven't got anything lying around, a lot of sewing shops sell little mixed packs of offcuts or fat quarters for just a few dollars.

Anchor

Cross stitch in two strands

Symbol	No.	Symbol	No.
~	002	⋈	243
/	006	0	275
△	055	+	293
♥	057	♡	305
★	108	S	314
≷	109	□	362
∩	120	◇	942
K	140	▲	1013
◆	146	★	1030
X	185	×	1092
#	187	Ξ	1094
@	241		

Backstitch in two strands

——	314
	chicks

Backstitch in one strand

——	236
	all other details

French knots in one strand

●	236
	eyes

Materials

Felt decorations

- 14 count aida, 15x18cm (6"x7¼") for each
- Pastel felt, 12x14cm (4¾"x5½") piece for each
- Glass beads
- Thin ribbons

Mix and match the charts to create the exact look you want

Sweet tooth

With six of these yummy cards to choose from, you can make one for everyone you know without feeling like you're repeating yourself!

Designed by: Diane Machin **Stitch time:** 6 hours each

Photography by Simon Lees

Materials

- 14 count white aida, 20x20cm (8"x8") for each design
- Patterned fabrics, 9.5x13.5cm (3¾"x5½") piece for each card
- Iron-on adhesive
- 3D foam pads
- White card, 15x22cm (6"x8") piece, folded

Why not stitch all six designs to create some cute party bunting that can be used year after year? Alternate between plain bunting flags and stitched ones

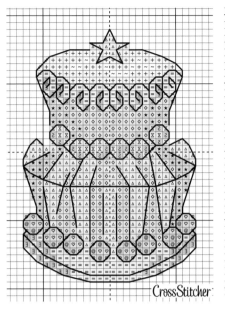

DMC	Anchor	Madeira
Cross stitch in two strands		
~ White	002	2402
0 Ecru	387	2404
★ 209	109	0711
◇ 210	108	0802
♡ 472	253	1414
@ 563	208	1207
Ǝ 602	057	0702
= 605	1094	0613
◧ 666	046	0210
△ 726	295	0109
□ 742	303	0114
⊠ 747	158	1104
Ƨ 955	203	1210
+ 3078	292	0102
Backstitch in one strand		
—— 317	400	1714
all details		

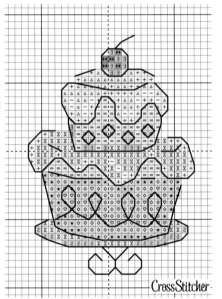

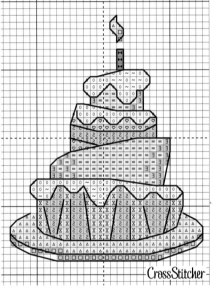

Backstitch a friend's name beneath the cake for a personal touch

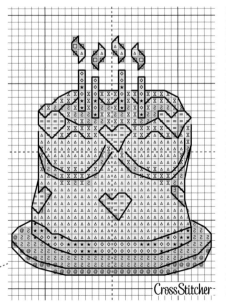

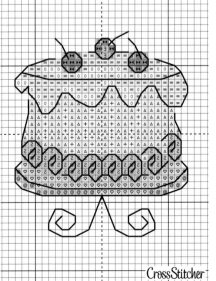

Make a...
birthday card

Step 1
BACK a piece of patterned fabric with iron-on adhesive. This will help give your fabric rigidity and keep it looking smooth. Cut out using pinking shears.

Step 2
REMOVE the paper backing and position the fabric onto your folded card. Carefully iron in place, directly on to the card.

Step 3
TRIM your stitching and back with white card. Attach to the center of your fabric patch using 3D foam pads.

Boudoir chic

This super-stylish lavender cushion oozes classic French charm – just add a few artfully placed mother-of-pearl buttons

Voilà – a fresh and feminine accessory for your bedroom that's full of a certain irresistible je ne sais quoi. Modeled on the minimalist, rustic style of French homeware this cushion and its matching lavender sachet will bring understated glamor to small or sparsely decorated rooms, and add a fascinating talking point to large or dramatic ones. The cushion is simple to make, and a few plain embellishments like wooden buttons or ribbon bows will add another interesting dimension.

Designed by: Lesley Teare
Design size: 15x15cm (6"x6")
Stitch time: 24 hours

Or try... **this!**
If you don't have time to make a cushion, how about a notebook cover?

A NOTEBOOK makes a great gift for any occasion, and a stitched cover is really simple to create – it just needs a bit of forward planning. Before you even start stitching, make sure you've got a large enough piece of fabric at the ready, because it will need to wrap around the back of the book as well. Measure the book you want the design to cover, and work out the best way of positioning the design on the front.

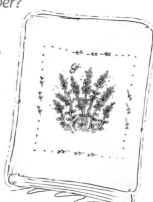

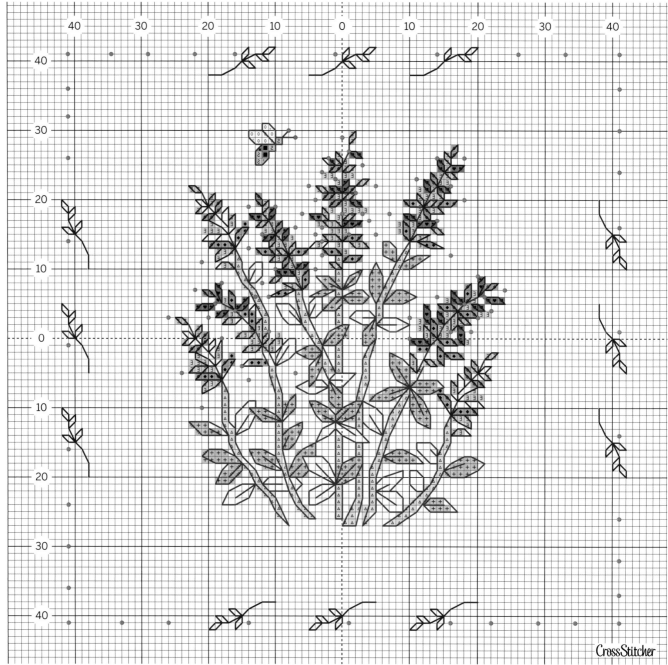

CrossStitcher

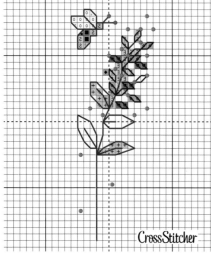

CrossStitcher

Materials

Cushion

- 28 count cream linen, 32x32cm (12¾"x12¾")
- Four 10mm (4") mother-of-pearl buttons
- Cream backing fabric, 32x32cm (12¾"x12¾")

Make a...
cushion and padded sachet

	DMC	Anchor	Madeira
Cross stitch in three strands			
Ǝ	155	109	0803
■	310	403	2400
♥	333	119	0903
△	524	858	1511
O	712	926	2101
+	3013	853	1605
◆	3746	1030	2702
S	3820	306	2509
Backstitch in one strand			
—	791	178	0904
lavender			
—	936	846	1507
all other details			
French knots in one strand			
●	936	846	1507
bee			
●	3746	1030	2702
lavender			

Step 1
TO MAKE your cushion, trim your stitching to measure 32x32cm (12¾"x12¾"). Fold and pin the edges under so your stitching measures 24x24cm (9½"x9½"). Repeat for your cream backing fabric.

Step 2
WITH right sides facing out, pin your two pieces of fabric together. Machine stitch 3cm (1") from the outside edges around three sides. Fill your cushion with stuffing before stitching the fourth side closed. Add mother-of-pearl buttons to finish.

Step 3
TO MAKE your sachet, cut your stitching and a piece of backing fabric to measure 11x13cm (4½"x5¼"). Make a double hem along the top edge of each piece. With right sides together, machine stitch in place along the remaining three sides. Fill with lavender and stuffing and tie closed with a length of twine.

Try to avoid trailing your threads across the back of your fabric. Dark or bright colored threads will create shadows across the front of your fabric where areas have been left unstitched. Always finish your thread off before moving on to the next area

20 COUNT ARIOSA
For a larger cushion, stitch your design on 20 count fabric instead. The finished result will give a more rustic, homespun look, and you can create a bigger cushion for large sofas and chairs.

Materials
Sachet
- 28 count cream linen, 15x15 cm (6"x6")
- Cream backing fabric, 11x13cm (4½"x5¼")
- Stuffing and lavender
- Twine

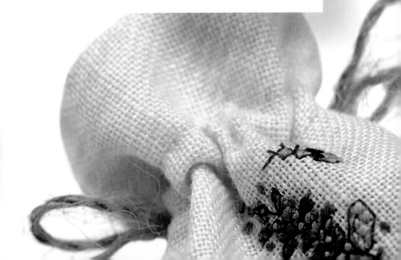

My best teacher

We remember good teachers for our whole lives, so show your thanks with this easy-to-stitch rustic set

Say thank you to a child's favorite teacher with this gorgeously classic sampler. If you haven't used linen before this is a good starter project, because it's stitched on 25 count rather than the slightly smaller and therefore harder to see 28 count. We've also thrown in a modern and fun extra – an individual stuffed and stitched apple that's quick and easy to stitch and makes a great accompaniment to a separate gift, or an alternative to a gift tag.

Designed by: Helen Philipps
Stitch time: 20 hours
Design size: 20x8cm (8"x3¼")

Instead of stitching 'Best Teacher' on your apple, use a basic backstitch alphabet to stitch the teacher's name

Materials

Apple sachet
- 14 count white aida, 18x18cm (7"x7")
- Backing fabric 15x15cm (6"x6")
- 14 count antique white aida, 8x7cm (3¼"x2¾"), for the tag
- Safety pin, ribbon and string

Picture
- 25 count linen, 40x25cm (16"x10")
- Painted frame

To Teach
is to
touch
a life
SCHOOL
forever

BEST Teacher

Photography by Jesse Wild

If you want a bolder look, stitch using three strands of cotton instead of two

DMC	Anchor	Madeira
Cross stitch in two strands		
✕ White	002	2401
～ Ecru	590	2101
✛ 223	895	0812
■ 317	400	1714
◇ 340	118	0902
♥ 347	1025	0407
♡ 349	9046	0212
△ 807	1039	1109
◆ 824	143	1010
▶◀ 839	1086	1913
Z 3047	853	2205
D 3052	262	1509
⧳ 3827	311	2012
☉ DMC Color Variations 4210		
Backstitch in one strand		
—— 317	400	1714
'best' lettering		
—— 839	1086	1913
all other details		

CrossStitcher

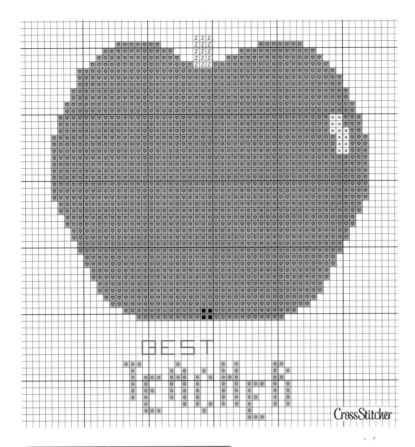

BEST

CrossStitcher

Make sure all your top crosses face the same way, and use an embroidery frame or hoop to stitch with

VARIATIONS

The lettering and border areas have been worked in DMC's Color Variations threads, which vary in color every 5cm (2"). To create a subtle color change, work each cross stitch individually, X X X, rather than working back and forth in rows of half cross stitch.

Make a... **framed picture**

Step 1

CUT a piece of mount card to fit the inside of the frame. For a raised effect, cut a piece of 2oz wadding to the same size and stick it to the mount with double-sided tape.

Step 2

PLACE your stitching centrally over the mount board and pin the fabric to secure. Start pinning from the center of each side outwards to help keep the design square to the board.

Step 3

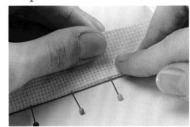

PLACE your stitching face down and stick double-sided tape on the reverse. Fold the excess material around the board and press firmly.

Step 4

SECURE the fabric edges with masking tape and remove the pins. Position in the frame and back with another piece of mount board. Finally, seal the edges of the frame with more masking tape.

CHRISTMAS

THE FESTIVE SEASON IS THE BUSIEST
TIME FOR PRESENTS, SO TAKE YOUR PICK
OF OUR GORGEOUS STOCKING FILLERS

Vintage childhood

We've given traditional 1950s Christmas scenes a contemporary overhaul for a card collection with lashings of Enid Blyton-style charm

Designed by: Maria Diaz **Stitch time:** 4 – 5 hours each

Photography by Philip Sowels

DMC	Anchor	Madeira
Cross stitch in two strands		
✕ B5200	001	2401
◪ 317	400	1714
♡ 320	215	1311
= 341	117	0901
♥ 347	1025	0407
5 368	214	1310
0 402	1047	2307
✕ 435	365	2010
∩ 436	363	2011
8 597	168	1110
2 598	167	1111
I 644	391	1814
> 676	887	2208
╲ 677	885	2207
◼ 792	941	0905
▲ 793	176	0906
3 950	4146	2309
✚ 3328	1024	0406
Backstitch in one strand		
— B5200	001	2401
snowflakes		
— 320	215	1311
lettering		
— 347	1025	0407
lettering		
— 413	236	1713
all other outlines and details		
— 783	307	2212
lettering		
— 792	941	0905
lettering		
French knots in one strand		
● 347	1025	0407
lettering		
● 413	236	1713
hats		
○ 747	158	1104
mistletoe		
● 783	307	2212
lettering		

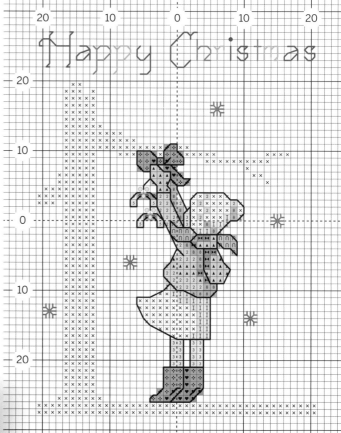

Materials

• 28 count cream linen, 15x15cm (6"x6")
• Cream cards, 12x15cm (4"x6")
• Corrugated card, 10x13cm (4"x5")

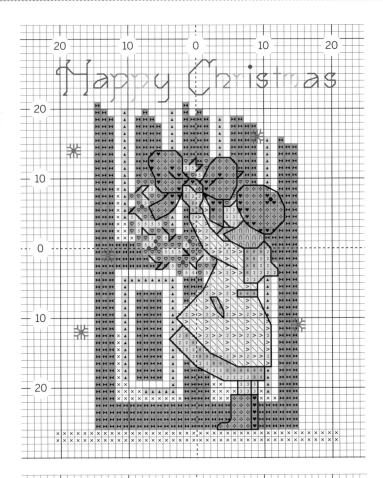

Happy Christmas

Seasons Greetings

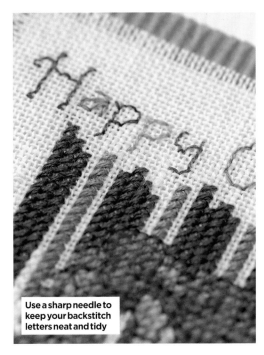

Use a sharp needle to keep your backstitch letters neat and tidy

Work the light areas first to prevent darker threads getting tangled up

For a smooth professional finish back your stitching with white card or paper before mounting on your corrugated card using double-sided tape

The holly & the ivy

Welcome your guests with a luxurious Christmas wreath – complete with easy to make stitched decorations that ooze festive style

With this hanging on your front door you'll have people lining up to come in and sample your brandy and mince pies. All you need is a plain wreath, some plastic canvas, a length of pretty ribbon, a bit of wire and a couple of skeins of your favorite color thread. Add a few baubles and other bits and bobs if you like too, for extra sparkle. If your front door is exposed to the elements, hang your wreath indoors so your cross stitch decorations won't get wet in the rain or snow.

Designed by: Diane Machin
Stitch time: 4 hours each

Or try... this!

Try a few different color options for the look you want

PURPLE: For a quirkier, contemporary feel, go for DMC 3834

WINTER TEAL: DMC 3809 is perfect for a more wintery look

BRIGHT RED: Choose DMC 304 to get a rich and traditional red

Materials
- 14 count plastic canvas, 10x10cm (4"x4") piece for each
- Wire

CrossStitcher

If you're not a fan of plastic canvas, try stitching your designs on 14 count white aida. Back with iron-on interfacing to add stiffness and keep the edges from fraying

CARDS & TAGS

If you don't want to make wreath decorations, stitch the designs as cards or gift tags instead. Pick some coordinating card to mount them on, and try stitching some of the areas in metallic thread for a nice shimmer.

Finishing **idea**
Pick the best wreath to show off your decs in style

FRESH WREATHS start to become available in November, but you could always invest in an artificial one instead. You can find them at lots of stores and these days there are lots of alternatives to plain green foliage. These simple designs will go with any color and style of wreath – just choose one with lots of branchy bits to dangle decs from.

DMC	Anchor	Madeira
Cross stitch in two strands		
✕ White	002	2402
◨ 414	235	1801
▢ 415	398	1802
♥ 947	330	0205
▬ DMC Light Effects E5200		
Backstitch in one strand		
— 414	235	1801
dove beak		
— 947	330	0205
snowman, star		
— DMC Light Effects E5200		
all other details		

How to… **attach wire**

SECURE a piece of wire to the back of each design by looping thread around the wire several times. Add a dab of glue to the center of the wire for security.

Stitch, craft & sew

Indulge in some traditional festive stitching and make a set of decorative sachets that will be treasured for years to come

Designed by: Anette Eriksson
Stitch time: 7 hours each

With rustic ribbon, felt backing and scented stuffing, these sachets are the decorations you've been waiting for!

DMC	Anchor	Madeira
Cross stitch in three strands		
319	1044	1313
320	215	1311
321	047	0510
367	216	1312
368	214	1310
644	391	1814
666	046	0210
816	043	0512
3801	1098	0411
3866	926	1901

Festive flourish

TRY MIXING a few spoonfuls of Christmasy spices such as cloves or potpourri in with your stuffing for a warm and homey scent! Then next year just add a drop of essential oil to freshen the scent!

Stitch it on aida! For an even quicker finish, try 14 count cream aida

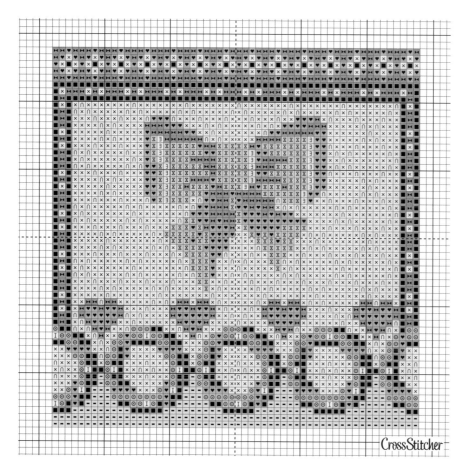

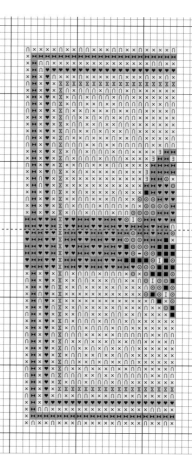

CrossStitcher

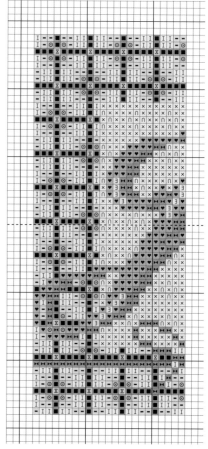

CrossStitcher

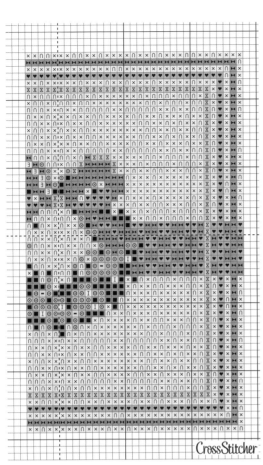

CrossStitcher

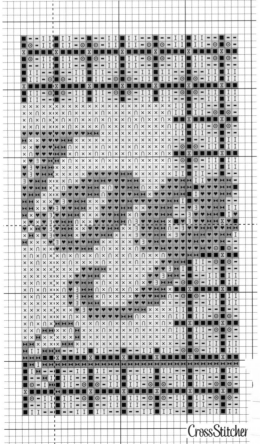

CrossStitcher

Make a...
padded sachet
Step 1

TRIM your stitched piece, leaving 2cm (¾") of excess all the way around. Cut a piece of dark green felt to the same size. With right sides facing, pin in place.

Step 2

SANDWICH a ribbon loop between the layers at the top of your sachet. Machine or hand stitch around the shape leaving an opening for turning.

Step 3

TURN RIGHT side out. Fill with stuffing and potpourri if you like. Slip stitch the opening closed and you're finished.

HIGH COLOR
Use three strands of thread instead of two to give the rich reds and greens in these designs for eye-popping impact.

Materials
- 24 count putty colored evenweave, 20x20cm (8"x8") for each
- Dark green felt, 15x15cm (6"x6")
- Ribbons
- Stuffing

	DMC	Anchor	Madeira
Cross stitch in three strands			
■	319	1044	1313
−	320	215	1311
♥	321	047	0510
⊙	367	216	1312
I	368	214	1310
∩	644	391	1814
X	666	046	0210
⋈	816	043	0512
Ǝ	3801	1098	0411
×	3866	926	1901

Your December Stitching Diary

Count down to Christmas Day with 25 quick designs you can make into tree decorations, festive table linen and gorgeous gift wrapping

25 PROJECTS STITCH EACH IN UNDER AN HOUR

We all know what it's like to get to Christmas Eve and suddenly realize some little card or gift has slipped through the net. Cue frantic panicking and late-night shopping trips! But not this year – because we've created this stylish collection of festive designs that you can stitch in just an hour and craft into beautiful gifts and decorations. And the great thing is, the making up part needn't be time consuming either – just gather up your spare bits of ribbon, felt and pretty papers, dig out glue and sticky tape, and start experimenting. Invest in some handy materials like 3D foam pads and garden twine for extra touches.

Designed by: Anette Eriksson

Finish your hanging sachets with blanket stitch edging – it's stylish and functional!

Materials

Felt sachets
- 28 count white evenweave
- 14 count white aida
- Purple felt scraps
- Ribbons and beads
- Stuffing

WHOLE STITCHES ONLY

DMC	Anchor	Madeira
Cross stitch in two strands		
★ 471	265	1501
♥ 550	101	0714
⊆ 917	089	0706
0 3348	264	1409
△ 3837	111	0713
Ǝ DMC Light Effects E3852		

CrossStitcher

Make... felt sachets

Their gorgeous handmade appeal makes them a chic alternative to shiny baubles

Step 1

CUT two felt shapes to the same size for each decoration. We've chosen a variety of squares, circles and heart shapes. Cut an aperture large enough to fit your stitched design in the middle of one of the pieces.

Step 2

ATTACH your stitching to the felt piece with small running stitches around the aperture. We used small stitches and coordinating thread, but for a bolder look, choose contrasting colored thread.

Step 3

SANDWICH thin white wadding or stuffing between the two felt layers. Add a blanket stitch around the outside edge to close. Turn to page 120 to learn how to work your blanket stitch edging.

Step 4

ATTACH a loop for hanging to the back of your sachet by looping purple thread around the cut ends. Sew a coordinating bead or button to the front of your sachet for the perfect finishing touch.

Alternate a stitched motif with a chunky button for a crafty, homemade look

Materials

Tableware
- 14 count waste or soluble canvas
- 14 count aida band
- 28 count white evenweave
- White linen napkins
- Buttons, ribbon and charms
- Papers and cardstock

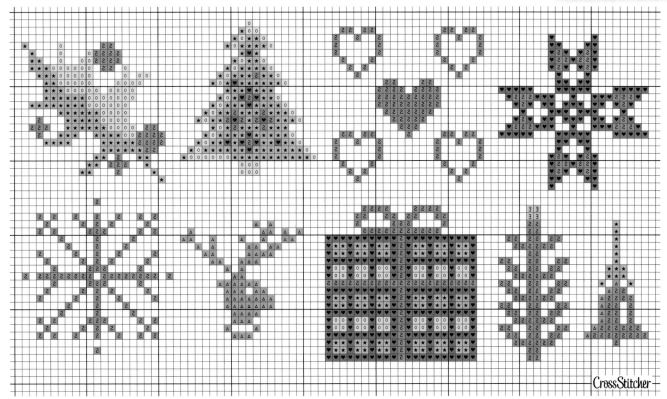

	DMC	Anchor	Madeira
Cross stitch in two strands			
★	471	265	1501
♥	550	101	0714
S	917	089	0706
0	3348	264	1409
△	3837	111	0713
E	DMC Light Effects E3852		

Try... **changing the colors**
Purple not your shade? No problem!

YOU CAN stitch these designs in whatever colors you like. If red is your thing, go for a more traditional scheme of scarlets and burgundies.

Or how about a wacky combination of black and hot pink? Add some metallic threads too for extra sparkle. Be creative!

©iStockphoto.com/Liliboas

WHOLE STITCHES ONLY

NAPKINS
Stitch a couple of motifs directly on to store-bought napkins using waste or soluble canvas. It's really easy to do!

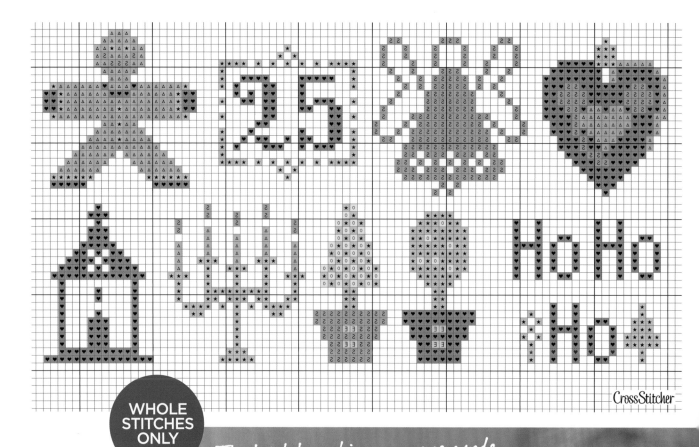

WHOLE STITCHES ONLY

CrossStitcher

The trick to making gorgeous cards, tags and bags is layering. Combine a variety of colors, shapes and textures for the greatest impact

Materials

Cards, tags and bags
• 28 count white evenweave
• 14 count white aida
• Papers and cardstock
• Pretty ribbons and cord
• Buttons, sequins and beads

Cooking up a storm

With this chic apron and oven mitts set you're guaranteed to have the best-dressed kitchen this Christmas. Now, where's that pudding recipe?

Why should the kitchen miss out on all the Christmas decorating fun? This stylish kitchenware set, inspired by Scandinavian stencil designs, is essential equipment for this year's festivities – when you're not wearing them, just display them where everyone passing through can see and admire them! Or if someone else is hosting Christmas this year, make a set as a gift for the chef. Just remember that these are functional items that will probably need a good long soak after the washing-up is done, so make sure you choose fabrics, threads and embellishments that won't come off or color-run in the washing machine.

Designed by: Lesley Teare
Stitch time: 4-6 hours each

We've stitched our designs directly onto calico fabric using waste canvas for a smooth finish

Or try... this!
Red isn't the only festive color option out there...

PURPLE: Stitch the designs with DMC 718 and choose a bright purpley-pink fabric to match

TEAL: DMC 3812 is an eye-popping green and will give you a classic set you can use all year round

Materials

- Plain colored apron and oven mitts
- Calico fabric
- Waste or soluble canvas

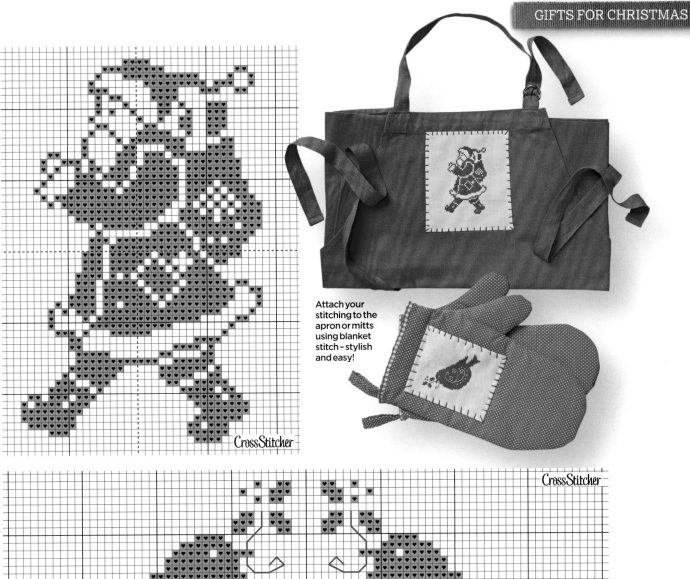

Attach your stitching to the apron or mitts using blanket stitch – stylish and easy!

CrossStitcher

CrossStitcher

	DMC	Anchor	Madeira
Cross stitch in two strands			
♥	321	047	0510
Backstitch in one strand			
—	White robin	002	2402
—	321 stems	047	0510

Finishing **touch**

IF YOU'RE a seasoned sewer you might find it easiest to make your own apron or oven mitts from scratch, so you can get the color, fabric and fit you want. But don't worry if that sounds too tricky for you – there are lots of places where you can buy plain, ready-made kitchen items to embellish with cross stitch.

These stencil-effect designs make great Christmas decorations too! To make a stocking, stitch onto felt, cut out two stocking shapes, add some ribbon trim and blanket stitch around the edges

Stitch it on aida!
For a super speedy finish, stitch your designs on 14 count cream aida instead.

How to... **blanket stitch**
A pretty and functional way to finish the raw edges of projects

Step 1

SECURE your thread on the reverse of your fabric and bring it up to the front to start stitching. Working from right to left, bring your needle back down a few millimeters away from where you came up.

Step 2

BEFORE pulling your thread all the way through, pass your needle through the thread loop to create your first stitch. Don't worry if your first stitch is more triangular in appearance than square – this is perfectly normal.

Step 3

TO MAKE your next stitch, take your needle down through the fabric. Before pulling all the way, pass your needle through the loop, working from back to front to create the stitch. Continue for each additional stitch.

Winter wonderland

We've got your Christmas cards covered with this chic selection of traditional and contemporary designs. Just pick your favorites and get stitching!

Designed by: Angela Poole

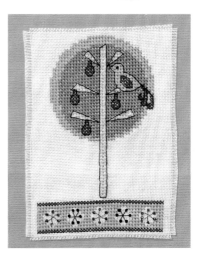

Swap our thread and fabric colors for your own choice to get the look you really want

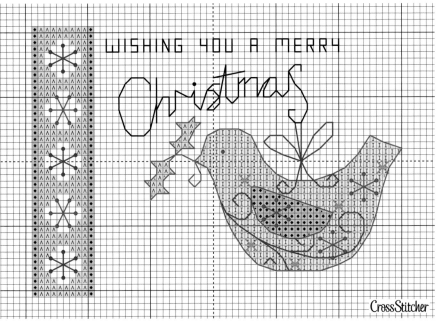

	Anchor	DMC	Madeira
Cross stitch in two strands			
◆	094	3834	0706
I	096	554	2713
✣	100	327	2714
⋈	102	550	2709
∧	185	959	1112
⊠	187	958	1114
⌐	1092	964	1104
K	DMC Light Effects E718		
∩	DMC Light Effects E747		
Backstitch in two strands			
——	102	550	2709
lettering			
Backstitch in one strand			
——	094	3834	2713
tree decorations			
——	102	550	2709
trees, animals, patterns			
——	188	3812	2706
tree, circle			
——	DMC Light Effects E718		
all other details			
——	DMC Light Effects E747		
bird and bauble borders			
——	DMC Light Effects E3843		
tree, baubles			
French knots in two strands			
●	102	550	2709
lettering			
French knots in one strand			
●	102	550	2709
eyes, stars, bird			
●	DMC Light Effects E718		
patterns			

CrossStitcher

PRETTY EDGING

For a stylish shabby-chic feel, fray the edges of your stitching when you cut the finished design out. If you're working on aida, trimming the edges with pinking shears is another nice way of adding texture. It's difficult to pink evenweave, though, so just pull a few strands out of the edges until you've got the frayed effect you want.

Materials

- 28 count white evenweave, 17x20cm (6¾"x8") for each
- Colored card, 14x20cm (5"x8"), folded in half
- White paper to back your design

Irresistible Gifts
to cross stitch

123

Gold coins

Bring the magic back to Advent with this adorable felt calendar that's guaranteed to be the talking point of your kids' playtime. The other moms will be begging you for the chart!

Start this Christmas craft early. Your kids are going to absolutely adore this Advent calendar, but you're going to need plenty of time to make it for them! The irresistible recipe of felt, chocolate coins and festive characters is sure to bring smiles to little faces, but if you don't want to tackle the whole design stitch the individual motifs onto gift tags or cards instead. Be really creative – just remember to buy lots of chocolate coins!

Designed by: Kerry Morgan

Stitch time: 27 hours

Design size: 22.3x22.3cm (8¾"x8¾")

Each of our pockets has been designed to fit an average-sized chocolate coin, but you can fill yours with any treats you like!

Materials

- 16 count rustic aida, 50x50cm (20"x20")
- Green felt, two 47x60cm (18½"x23¾") pieces
- Red and yellow felt, see step-by-step for sizing
- Cotton or polyester wadding, two 42x55cm (16½"x21¾") pieces
- Red bobble trim, 50cm (20")
- Green and yellow sewing thread

Photography by Neil Godwin

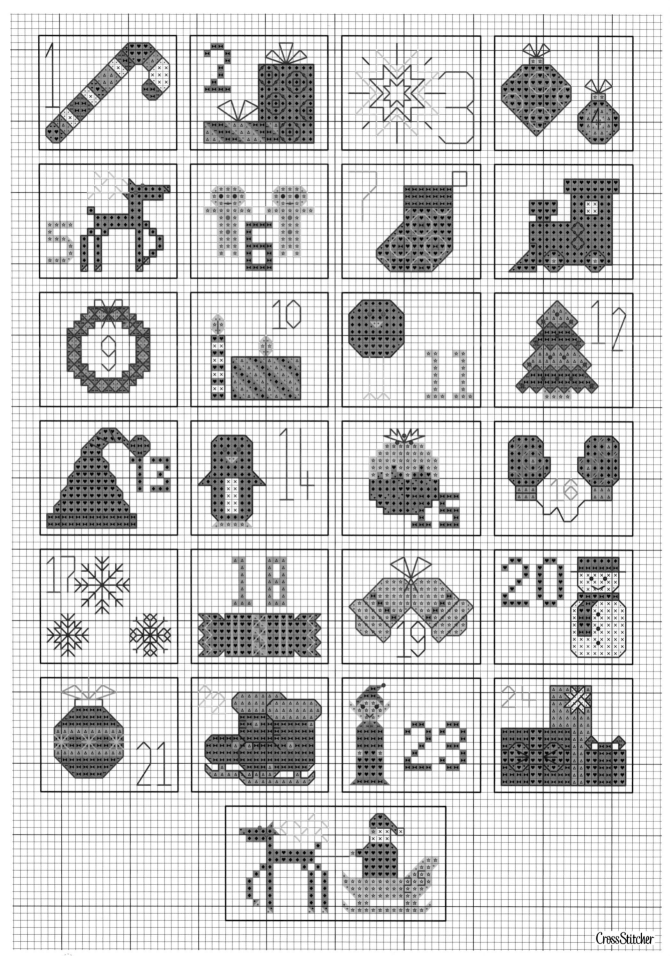

CrossStitcher

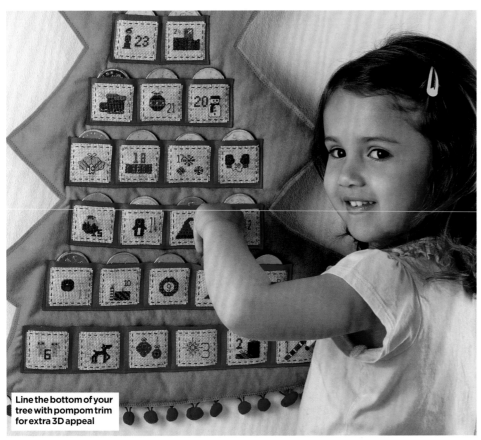

Line the bottom of your tree with pompom trim for extra 3D appeal

	DMC	Anchor	Madeira
Cross stitch in two strands			
✕ White	002		2402
♥	321	047	0510
◨	505	211	1206
△	988	243	1402
☆	728	306	0113
◆	797	132	0912
Backstitch in one strand **Numbers in two strands**			
▬	321	047	0510
▬	505	211	1206
▬	988	243	1402
▬	728	306	0113
▬	797	132	0912
French knots in one strand			
●	321	047	0510
elf hat, holly berries, tree			
●	505	211	1206
penguin, reindeer and bird eyes, gingerbread men			
●	797	132	0912
elf, gingerbread men and snowman eyes			
Guide lines			
▬	Use as a guide for cutting out patches		

Instead of pre-cutting your aida pieces, stitch all 25 motifs on a single piece of 50x50cm (20"x20") aida. Stitch each one with about 4cm (1") of space around it

TRY BUTTONS
Why not try replacing a few of your motifs with colorful Christmas themed buttons?

Make an...
Advent tree

Step 1
BEGIN by trimming each motif into pieces 4.5cm (1¾") wide and 4cm (1½") tall. Fray the outer row of aida blocks around each piece. Cut the '25' motif into a 4x6cm (1½"x2½") piece. Cut your red felt strips to these measurements: 5x32cm (2"x12½"), 5x26.5cm (2"x10½"), two 5x21cm (2"x8¼") strips, 5x15.5cm (2"x6"), 5x10.5cm (2"x4") and 5x6.5cm (2"x2½").

Step 2
USING a red running stitch, attach your stitched motifs to the red felt. Moving from left to right, attach motifs 6, 5, 4, 3, 2 and 1 to the longest strip. Attach 11, 10, 9, 8 and 7 to the second longest strip. Continue in this way until you've reached motif 25, which should be attached to the smallest felt piece.

Step 3
CUT two pieces of green felt into your desired tree shape. Your tree should be be at least 44cm (17½") wide at the base and at least 55cm (21¾") tall. Make sure your stitched strips fit into the tree shape before you start cutting. Next cut two pieces of thin wadding, just slightly smaller than the felt shape.

Step 4
WITH right sides facing out, sandwich the wadding between the two pieces of felt and sew a zig zag stitch around the entire outside of the tree using green thread. You can also work this by hand using running or blanket stitch. If necessary, trim away any wadding that may be showing through.

Step 5
CREATE the star in the same way as your tree. Arrange your red felt and stitched strips to the tree until you're happy with the placement. Stitch around each design, leaving the top open. This will give you a 5cm (2") wide pocket for each design, the perfect size for a chocolate coin! Attach pompom trim to the bottom edge of your tree and a ribbon for hanging at the top.

**Cross Stitched Cards for
Special Occasions**
ISBN 978-1-57421-376-8 **$9.99**
DO3500

Love Patchwork
ISBN 978-1-57421-446-8 **$14.99**
DO5414

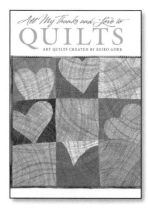

**All My Thanks and
Love to Quilts**
ISBN 978-1-57421-425-3 **$24.99**
DO5396

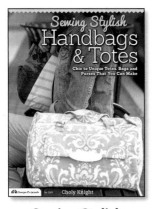

**Sewing Stylish
Handbags & Totes**
ISBN 978-1-57421-422-2 **$22.99**
DO5393

**Making Jewelry with
T-Shirt Yarn**
ISBN 978-1-57421-374-4 **$8.99**
DO3498

Joy of Zentangle
ISBN 978-1-57421-427-7 **$24.99**
DO5398

Sew Baby
ISBN 978-1-57421-421-5 **$19.99**
DO5392

Felt from the Heart
ISBN 978-1-57421-365-2 **$9.99**
DO3488

Parachute Cord Craft
ISBN 978-1-57421-371-3 **$9.99**
DO3495